ABOUT FREDERICK BUECHNER

Frederick Buechner brings the reader to his knees, sometimes in laughter, sometimes in an astonishment very close to prayer, and at the best of times in a combination of both.

The New York Times Book Review

With profound intelligence, Buechner's novel does what the finest, most appealing literature does: it displays and illuminates the seemingly unrelated mysteries of human character and ultimate ideas . . . One of our finest writers.

Annie Dillard, *Boston Globe*

If Frederick Buechner subordinated his nature and chose to write on naughts and nothings, he would still exalt his readers. When he is in representative harmony and writes of the accessibility of God to humanity and of humanity's agreement with its potential divinity, we, the readers, are lifted up, buoyed up, and promised wholeness.

Maya Angelou

You don't have to be in the habit of going to church to listen to such a literary minister; you don't have to be a believer to be moved by Mr. Buechner's faith.

John Irving

Frederick Buechner is a beacon. When we can't remember what is true and what it all means, he's the person we turn to.

Anne Lamott

Frederick Buechner has inspired me not only with his writing, but with his generosity of spirit. I'm incredibly thankful.

Rachel Held Evans

He isn't trying to persuade—he's trying to understand what he himself believes and thinks. And that honesty is more persuasive than the most polished argument.

John Ortberg

Frederick Buechner doesn't just show us how to write; he shows us how to live.

Philip Yancey

Frederick Buechner is not just a wordsmith but an imagesmith—he's the bridge between Gutenberg and Google.

Len Sweet

To each new generation, his work is a revelation.

The Lutheran

Frederick Buechner gives new life to Christian truth.

Katelyn Beaty

He raises the bar not only for Christian writers, but for all of literature.

Mako Fujimura

THE
REMARKABLE
ORDINARY

Also by Frederick Buechner

THE
REMARKABLE
ORDINARY

How to Stop, Look, and Listen to Life

FREDERICK
BUECHNER

ZONDERVAN
BOOKS

ZONDERVAN BOOKS

The Remarkable Ordinary
Copyright © 2017 by Frederick Buechner Literary Assets, LLC

Published in Grand Rapids, Michigan, by Zondervan. Zondervan is a registered trademark of The Zondervan Corporation, L.L.C., a wholly owned subsidiary of HarperCollins Christian Publishing, Inc.

Requests for information should be addressed to customercare@harpercollins.com.

ISBN 978-0-310-35190-0 (softcover)
ISBN 978-0-310-35163-4 (audio)
ISBN 978-0-310-35252-5 (ebook)

Art direction: Curt Diepenhorst
Interior design: Denise Froehlich
Zondervan Editorial: John Sloan, Robert Hudson, Gwyneth Findlay

Printed in the United States of America

24 25 26 27 28 LBC 32 31 30 29 28

CONTENTS

FOREWORD

The issuing of a new Frederick Buechner book began as a project three years ago. Some of his unpublished 1987 Norton and 1990 Laity Lodge lecture materials were the well from which this volume, *The Remarkable Ordinary*, would spring. If it's one thing publishers of Frederick Buechner hear, it is whether there is more that he has written. The answer is now yes.

Most book jackets for Buechner say something like this: Frederick Buechner's books have been translated into twenty-seven languages. He has been called a "major talent" by the *New York Times* and "one of our finest writers." He has been a finalist for the Pulitzer Prize and the National Book Award.

What those jackets don't say is what Buechner does on the page, as far as inspiration, as far as hope, as far as faith.

Frederick Buechner is a writer for devout skeptics and loyal believers. Those who read him find out that while he believes in a God who works in the ordinary world, he understands why there are questions as to why he doesn't unleash his extraordinary powers into a hurting world. He wonders with the reader and does not condemn. But he does seek out God's mystery and his power. And he finds both, in the common things and in the painful things.

Buechner writes with the brush of an artist about things we know and think we know. The things we have heard over and over in church, and now seem worn and tired, Buechner makes fresh and gives new angles to find even more depth.

Buechner writes about grace and beauty, love and hope, darkness and light, tragedy and blessing, despair and joy . . . But he does so in a way that is unexpected, freshly creative, not bound in time, sometimes outrageous, sometimes scandalous, but always speaking about the God we know we can believe in.

Now to the subject of this book. Frederick Buechner shows the reader how to stop, look, and listen to life. He reflects on the connection between art and faith, and how both teach us how to pay attention to the remarkableness of our lives, to watch for the greatness in the ordinary, and to use our imaginations to see the greatness in others and love them well. As we begin to stop, look, and listen to our lives and what God is doing in them, we begin to uncover the plot of our life's story. And as we learn where the plot is taking us in our search for meaning and peace, we finally have the eyes to catch glimpses of joy through our devotion and prayer.

Anyone familiar with Buechner's writings, particularly his memoirs, will already know about his father's suicide and his family's attempts to deal with that tragic loss; indeed, his father's death haunts much of Buechner's writing, and he tells the story over and over again throughout his books. This book is no different, but in the lectures from which this book is derived, he tells his story in a more personal way, giving us a slightly different lens through which to view tragedy and God's presence within it.

As my fellow colleague and editor Caleb Seeling and I reflected about the content of this book, we began to feel that though it is about the ordinary things of life, it is not an ordinary book. It is not ordinary because it points to the extraordinary that we can find in every day we wake, in every discussion we have, in every walk we take, in every moment we come upon.

Many times we say life is typical, mundane, common, routine, or dull. Buechner convinces us that every moment is worth it. Our steps are all the beginnings of a walk into a hall of art, life, and meaning that will never disappoint.

JOHN SLOAN
EDITOR

INTRODUCTION

I am haunted now as I never was before by the sense that we all of us have the mark of God's thumb upon us. We have the image of God within us. We have a holy place within us that gets messed up in a million ways. But it's there, and more and more I find myself turning inward toward that and trying to learn how to be quiet. Someone once gave me a book called *Creative Silence*, and I thought, *Oh, that's just what I need.*

So I'm writing, I suppose, hoping to get another few steps in that direction, toward turning off the eternal chatter, the endless dialogue that goes on inside most of us. Or at least, I can speak only for myself, to stop those words and just to exist somehow in the fullness and unspeakableness of the present and to let whatever is down in the holy place drift up.

In that hymn "Be Thou My Vision," there's one verse I love:

> Be Thou my buckler, my sword for the fight;
> Be Thou my dignity, Thou my delight;
> Thou my soul's shelter, Thou my high tower:
> Raise Thou me heavenward, O power of my power.

And maybe that suggests some sort of a theme to find that vision within—to live out of that inner holy place.

FREDERICK BUECHNER

THE
REMARKABLE
ORDINARY

PART 1

STOP, LOOK, AND LISTEN FOR GOD

CHAPTER 1

THE
REMARKABLE
ORDINARY

It has been my experience that at a cocktail party or any sort of social occasion, the conversation usually works around at some point to somebody asking, "What do you do?" And I always envy the person who can answer that simply by saying, I'm a computer expert, or a farmer, or a dietitian, or a sausage stuffer, or what have you. When it comes to me, I have no easy answer to that question. I always stumble over it. I usually start by saying I'm a minister, which is what I think I basically am. The next question, of course, is "Where is your church?" And then I have to say, "Well, I don't have any church." And you can almost always see sort of a glaze go over the eyes of people. And the following question is apt to be "If you don't have a church, what do you do?" and when I say, "I write books," very often their eyes turn up so you can only see the whites of their eyes. They are confused by that. Life is confusing. A minister should have a church, and a writer should write books, and the two are separate and so on, and to have somebody doing both is somehow hard to focus on. I understand that reaction because, in a way, it is hard for me to focus on.

I made the decision when I was at Union Seminary not to go on and be a regular church minister but to write books, and it was a hard decision to make. I remembered people like Gerard Manley Hopkins who, when he went Jesuit, took all of the poems he'd written up to that point and burned them because he figured he was going to give his life to Christ. To him, it meant giving *everything* to Christ. And I know what that means, and I still feel somewhere deep within me a little bit of that, but not much, because I've decided that writing books is a kind of ministry, a sort of weird kind, but a kind. And I also decided that art and religion, though the people whose eyes roll up in their heads don't immediately think so, have a great deal to do with each other. They're both working in very much the same ways and to very much the same end. To explore this idea, let's first look at what art at its best really does.

■ ■ ■

Consider first of all the simplest, most minimal form of literature I know, a haiku—those little seventeen-syllable poems that grew out of that form of Japanese Buddhism known as Zen and became popular in this country in the '50s and '60s. What I love about the form is that lots of things that literature usually does, haiku don't do at all, but what they do do, I think, is what all literature does. Let me just run one haiku by you. It's not among my favorites, but it's apparently the most famous haiku, and anybody who knows them knows this by heart. It's by the seventeenth-century haiku master Matsuo Bashō:

> An old silent pond.
> Into the pond a frog jumps.
> Splash. Silence again.

Read it again:

> An old silent pond.
> Into the pond a frog jumps.
> Splash. Silence again.

As I said, what I love about this haiku is that so much of what literature normally does is not being done here. The language could hardly be more commonplace. Simple words. Only three of them have more than one syllable. The subject could hardly be more pedestrian. Simply walking along the edge of a pond, frightening a frog who jumps into the pond, then the noise of the splash, and then the return of the silence.

The whole genius of haiku is that they don't mean anything. People who try to figure out what a haiku means are beating up the wrong path. The frog doesn't stand for anything. The pond doesn't stand for anything. The splash has no symbolic value or anything like that. All of these things that other literature might be attempting are not attempted by the haiku at all. The haiku settles for doing, as I read it anyway, one very simple but very crucial thing—it tries to put a frame around the moment. It simply frames a moment. Of course, as soon as you put a frame around anything, you set it off, you make it visible, you make it real. Haiku enable us to see, to experience, this moment that is framed, and in this case, as I say, the most commonplace kind of moment of walking along, the frog plops, the silence comes back, and so on. If you and I had been along by the side of the pond, the chances are we wouldn't even have noticed the frog jumping into the water. We have other things on our mind. We have a place we're going and a place we've come from, other things are happening, your head itches, a cloud passes over the sun. We wouldn't have noticed it, perhaps, or if we had noticed it, chances are we would've dismissed it by naming it. Just a frog jumping into a pond. We do that all of the time, I think. We name it out of existence. Or we think about it. Maybe we'd think about it sickly, like that phrase in *Hamlet*: "Is sicklied o'er with the pale cast of thought." We'd have thought it out of its reality.

But what the haiku does is simply to say, no, no, no, don't do any of those things, don't think about it. Don't name it, just experience it. Hear it, see it, smell it, participate in it. I think that is what all literature, basically, is doing.

Writing does a lot of other things, of course. People write books to instruct. They write books to move us, to scare us, to enlighten us in all sorts of ways. But basically what these works of literature or of art are doing is to say, *Stop thinking*. Stop expecting. Stop living in the past. Stop living in the future. Stop doing anything and just pay attention to *this*. To this boy and this black man floating down the Mississippi River on a raft, this old king going crazy on a heath because two of his three daughters have done terrible things to him; pay attention to this young woman named Anna Karenina who is about to drop in front of a train because her love has failed her. Literature, before it is saying anything else, is saying, Be mindful. Stop whatever else you're doing and notice. Allow yourself to be seized by this, whether it's the frog, or the king, or the black man on the raft.

■ ■ ■

Not only, I think, does writing, in a way, ask us to stop, but it also enables us to stop. One of the things I'm always looking for in my old age is a way to stop the chatter that goes on inside of all of us. Of course any book that really works for you stops that chatter. It enables you to escape—for as long as you're reading it, as long as you're grasped by it—the confines of being you. You can sort of cast off the uniform of your own flesh in some funny way and put on the uniform of somebody else's skin. You can escape the little world that's inside your skin and live inside the world that the writer produces for you. It can be an escape in a frivolous sense, just escaping from you—which is not to be sneezed at, it's rather nice to have happen—but escaping from you into something richer, realer, more immediate, and more shimmering, even if it's only the moment of the frog jumping into the pond. Or a prayer, like the one I heard in a little staff meeting. Everybody was praying at the end of it, it was marvelous, but then a man started singing his prayer and it was at that instance like a work of art. I was so caught up in it. The shimmeringness of it, the un-repeatable-ness of it, the un-verbalizable-ness of it.

So, art is saying *Stop*. It helps us to stop by putting a frame around something and makes us see it in a way we would never have seen it under the normal circumstances of living, as so many of us do, on sort of automatic pilot, going through the world without really seeing much of anything.

■ ■ ■

It's even easier to see this, I think, in the case of painting—that art where the painter literally puts a frame around something. And you can think of whatever painting you choose to think of. My wife and I recently went to this marvelous exhibit of Monet, our favorite impressionist, and there's that marvelous series of paintings of a haystack out in some field in France. If you've ever seen those, you know what I'm talking about. Just a simple sort of haystack-shaped haystack, but painted in dawn, painted in rain, painted with frost and snow, painted at dusk, painted in such a way that this totally ordinary object simply shimmers with life, shimmers with suchness. It's not asking you to go anywhere away from that haystack. Just to see it. To see the miracle of it.

This is particularly true, it seems to me, in the case of great portraits, the way in which a face is framed in a way to make it unforgettable. And to me the great portraitist of all is Rembrandt. I remember as a child going to my grandparents who lived not far from the Metropolitan Museum in New York and going there again and again. He's so good, and I think especially of one portrait—I wish I could name it for you but I can't—of an old Dutch woman in a black dress and a tight-fitting white cap and a starched ruff and a sort of waxy pale skin, wrinkled, her upper teeth are gone, her lip is sunken in, her hands folded looking out from that frame. In no sense a remarkable face. If you saw that face sitting across the aisle from you on an airplane, or if you saw it coming down pushing a cart full of groceries, you'd never notice it at all. Not a remarkable face, but a face that has been so remarkably seen by Rembrandt that we are jolted into seeing it remarkably. And that old woman's face somehow becomes all faces. And all faces are somehow contained in that face.

And what I think the artist, the painter is doing, as the writer is saying *Stop*, the painter is saying *Look*, look at each other's faces the way Rembrandt looked at the old woman's face. Or look at your own face, maybe that's the hardest of all, in the mirror the way that Rembrandt looked at that old woman's face, which is to say look at it not just for the wrinkles and the sunken upper lip and the white ruff, but look at it for what lies within the face, for the life that makes the face the way it is.

You'd think that would be easy. It's so easy to look and see what we pass through in this world, but we don't. If you're like me, you see so little. You see what you expect to see rather than what's there.

When I was at Princeton, a psychology class conducted an experiment to make this point to people. There was a room that you peeked at through a little hole, and they told you what to look for—a position of a certain object and so on—and you would come away having looked through the peephole and answer questions about what you saw. Then they would ask, "Did you notice anything else about the room?" And people for the most part said, "No, we didn't." Well, the room was a crazy room. One wall was that high and the other wall was that high, and the ceiling went this way, and the floor went that way, but they didn't see that because they hadn't been told to expect to see that.

I've often thought too that if an angel appeared at this moment and outspread his golden wings, the chance would be that none of us would see it. Who expects to see an angel stretch out his golden wings? Remember that old *Candid Camera* show? The thing that fascinated me about it was so often some totally impossible thing would happen, like a car driving down the street with no driver in it or the parrot in the dry cleaner's shop making remarks about the World Series. Or I remember once a man was sitting in a restaurant and the flower on his table leaned over and sipped his Coca-Cola. What happened again and again was when people were confronted with these impossible situations, they did not see them, or they pretended not to see them, because life is confusing enough.

So, to help us out of our blindness, part of what the painter is doing is saying, *See what's there, not what you expect to see. See what is really present in your life. See yourself, see each other.*

■ ■ ■

And then music, whatever music is—I don't really know what music is, it's sound—but it seems to me the medium of music is basically time, whereas the medium of painting is space. In a painting you put one thing next to another thing, put the blue background next to the red heart on the wall, and so on. But the musician doesn't deal in space; he deals in time, one note follows another note the way one moment follows another moment, the way tock follows tick. And I think that what the musician is trying to do is to say, *Listen to time, pay attention to time, pay attention to the sounds and the silences of time. Experience the richness of time.*

The Greeks with their wonderful gift for distinctions made that distinction, which anybody who's ever gone to theological seminary knows well, between *Chronos* time—chronological time, watch time, calendar time, time to eat, time to go home—on the one hand and *Kairos* time on the other, which is not time thought of quantitatively, but rather qualitatively—it was a good time, it was a sad time, the time had come to do something, a confusing time. And I think what the musician, or what music, is doing at its best is to say, *Pay attention to the quality of time, to the Kairos time.* I even amuse myself sometimes, because I'm a verbal person, by trying to put words to what it is that a particular composer is trying to have us hear about time.

I've listened to a lot of Bach lately. We went to a wonderful Bach Festival in Bethlehem, Pennsylvania, this spring and heard the Christmas oratorio and those great plumes of music.

And it seems to me that Bach is saying, *Listen to the grandeur of time, listen to the stateliness of time.* Or Mozart . . . Karl Barth once said something about when the angels of God appear before the throne of grace, they're all singing Bach, but when they chatter among each other, it's all Mozart. Whatever Mozart is saying— there's a phrase in Mozart that I hear in everything I've ever heard of him almost, a plaintive little *la-da da da.* The *poignance* of time maybe, I don't know. And Debussy, the strange sort of *illuminess* of time, whatever word you want.

But each one of these composers is saying, *Pay attention to the quality of time. The Kairos-ness of time.* And in a way I think of the phrase *keep time.* You can think of keeping time in the normal sense as keeping to the meter of music, but music, in a way, is saying keep time in another way—keep it, keep in touch with it, keep your hands on it somehow. Keep in touch with the sadness of your own time, with the joy of time, with the marvelousness of time, with the terror of time, with the emptiness of time, with the fullness of time.

It is also saying, *Listen to the sounds, listen to the music of your own life.* Listen to the voices of the people you live with, listen to the songs that they sing. I don't mean the song they sing— tra-la-la—but I mean listen to the music of their voices. Listen to the slamming of the screen door. Listen to the patter of feet walking back up the path. Listen to the turning of a tap in the tub, because that is in a very profound and touching way the music of your life. It is the song out of time that sings to you. Keep in touch with time, not just as rush and tumble.

I think of rivers I've known. A lot of the time the river's surface is white, it's tumbling over rocks, but then it reaches a bend maybe, or a deep place, and then suddenly the surface stills and you can see down through it to the bottom, and what the music is saying, I think, is learn to do that somehow, to move yourself away from the tumble, the rush, the surface of time, chronological time, time as an everflowing stream, and look deep into time for whatever it is that lies at the heart of it, whatever quality it is, the mystery of time.

And ballet, I wasn't going to mention ballet because I don't know any more about it than I do these other arts, even less— but my wife and I went to Saratoga, which is near us in New York, where they have this one little performing arts center, and we saw the City Ballet do a couple of wonderful dances, one on Bach's Goldberg Variations. And I realized this art is working in both time *and* space. It's both music and it's spatial on the stage, and it's saying *listen* to this time, right now, and look, *look* at what you're looking at, look at the language the body speaks, the language the face speaks, the language the hands speak, these wonderful things the young, supple, beautiful bodies are doing up there on the stage to the music. These are the kind of things we all of us do less young-ly, less supple-y, less beautifully, but with our hands, with our bodies—pay attention to that. So generally—and this is not a complicated point, God knows—the arts frame our life for us so that we will experience it. Pay attention to it.

■ ■ ■

The nearest big town to us in Vermont is Rutland—it's not all that big, but big enough. To get to Rutland from where I live you go through a tiny little town called Wallingford. I've made that trip six billion times and have often found myself, when I'm driving alone, asking myself, "Now, have I been through Wallingford yet or not?" I can't remember. I find out only when I've gotten to a certain point, and I think, "Oh, here I am at

Rutland. I must've gone through Wallingford!" My point, not altogether a comic one, is that if somebody had taken a photograph of me as I was going through Wallingford, they would've taken a photograph of a human being who was not at that moment living his life. I was not present inside of my skin then. I did not see anything because I was so caught up in an inner dialogue.

So, stop and see. Become more sensitive, more aware, more alive to our own humanness, to the humanness of each other. Look with Rembrandt's eye, listen with Bach's ear, look with X-ray eyes that see beneath the surface to whatever lies beneath the surface.

I think the writer who first led me to see with X-ray eyes, to think in those terms, was J. D. Salinger—that mysterious old man who hadn't published anything for years before his death in 2010. But he wrote some marvelous books, and in *The Catcher in the Rye*, one of the things that I remember best is the protagonist Holden Caulfield, that poor, lost, confused little preppy who makes his way through Manhattan to wherever he thinks he's going. He runs into a lot of characters, some of whom are unpleasant: There's the pimp in the hotel who tries to bring him a girl, and he doesn't want the girl, and the pimp beats him up. He goes to a nightclub and there's a black pianist who plays very well, but he's become a professional black pianist—his true blackness is lost, and he's sort of playing the game; he's a phony. There are other characters like that who play a sort of negative role in his life, but Holden Caulfield says again and again, "I miss old so-and-so, I miss the pimp, I miss the phony black pianist," as if he sees beneath the phoniness, beneath the crookedness, beneath whatever it was about this person that was unpleasant and negative to something touching and human and to be missed, as if the party wouldn't have been complete even without old so-and-so.

And then of course, supremely in *Franny and Zooey*, the ability to see more than meets the eye. That book is really twin stories that were published together about the Glass children. The Glass children were on a radio quiz program called "It's a Wise Child" where they would answer questions. Through their experience on the show, Zooey learns to see with X-ray eyes from her brother Seymour:

> Seymour'd told me to shine my shoes just as I was going out the door with Walker. I was furious. The studio audience were all morons, the announcer was a moron, the sponsors were morons, and I just damn well wasn't going to shine my shoes for them, I told Seymour. I said they couldn't see them *anyway*, where we sat. He said to shine them anyway. He said to shine them for the Fat Lady. I didn't know what the hell he was talking about, but he had a very Seymour look on his face, and so I did it. He never did tell me who the Fat Lady was, but I shined my shoes for the Fat Lady every time I ever went on the air again—all the years you and I were on the program together, if you remember. I don't think I missed more than just a couple of times. This terribly clear, clear picture of the Fat Lady formed in my mind. I had her sitting on this porch all day, swatting flies, with her radio going full-blast from morning till night. I figured the heat was terrible, and she probably had cancer, and—I don't know. . . .
>
> But I'll tell you a terrible secret—Are you listening to me? *There isn't anyone out there who isn't Seymour's Fat Lady.* . . . There isn't anyone *anywhere* that isn't Seymour's

Fat Lady. . . . And don't you know—*listen* to me, now—*don't you know who that Fat Lady really is?* . . . Ah, buddy. Ah, buddy. It's Christ Himself. Christ Himself, buddy.[1]

Then there's that wonderful passage in C. S. Lewis's *Letters to Malcolm* where Lewis speaks of having met a European minister who had seen Hitler. Lewis says, "What'd he look like? What did Hitler look like?" and the minister says, "Like Christ, of course." Like Christ. Tremendously moving.

Our secret face is that face. Paul's right—the whole creation is moving, the whole great complex show has started so that we may eventually obtain the measure of the stature of the fullness of Christ, but to see it, the artist says, you have to stop and really *look*, look for it with X-ray eyes.

So there's a quick run-through of the arts, and the question is, what's it all got to do with religion? Stop, look, listen—a lot, I think. I think in a sense that is what biblical faith is saying almost before it says anything else: *Stop*, and *look*, and *listen*.

CHAPTER 2

TO SEE IS TO LOVE, TO LOVE IS TO SEE

When religions like Buddhism and Hinduism look at the world, they see an illusion. Impermanence. Something that has come into being almost by accident. Something circular. The great wheel of the universe that goes around and around and around—you were born only to die and only to be reborn, only to die again. The whole point of those Eastern religions is that the world is to be escaped. That's what Nirvana is: the snuffing out, the final relinquishing of this awful grasp you will have on the wheel of life into this ineffable bliss of whatever Nirvana might be, something quite different from life. Creation is an accident, the creation of a dream that ultimate reality dreamed. It has no permanence. It has no purpose. It has nothing of any lasting value.

Not true with the Christian faith. The biblical faith says creation is of enormous importance because God created it. He made it, he sustains it, he speaks in it, he moves in it. He sent the Christ into it, who walked on it, who got sick from it, who ate on it, who wanted a job on it, who preached on it, who loved on it, who died on it. It is of enormous importance. Pay attention to it. It is crucial. Souls are lost and souls are saved in this world; therefore live, watch, pay attention to it as if your life depended on it because, of course, your life does depend upon it. It seems to me almost before the Bible says anything else, it is saying that—how important it is to be alive and to pay attention to being alive, pay attention to each other, pay attention to God as he moves and as he speaks. Pay attention to where life or God has tried to take you.

The prophets were also saying to pay attention, especially to history. Pay attention especially to what's going on in the headlines, with Amos, for instance, thundering out, Pay attention to the way the rich exploit the poor, to the way there are people living off the fat of the land in air-conditioned bedrooms and more to eat than they can handle while there are other people who are starving to death, who are sleeping in the streets of New York and San Antonio and God knows where in bags and cardboard boxes. Pay attention to that, says Amos, because God is speaking a terrible word through that, of judgment and of wrath, and of hope, in a way. Or the prophet Isaiah, who says, Watch the foreign policy of the nation, read those headlines, the powers in the north are coming to punish Israel for her running off after foreign gods every chance she has, and so on.

These prophetic voices continue, of course, and sometimes history itself becomes prophetic. I remember watching those students holding demonstrations in Tiananmen Square in Beijing, and there was a period when the students were being gentle, and the soldiers were being gentle, nobody was shooting, and nobody was shouting, and something so precious was starting, was trying to happen. I thought I could hardly watch without tears in my eyes. And then, of course, the shooting did start, and the tanks rolled in, and the bodies fell, and some were arrested, and here history itself was saying, *Pay attention to what's happening because these are the prophetic words being spoken to you on your television screen about the kingdom at hand.*

Pay attention not just to the mighty acts that get into the headlines, but *pay attention* to the mighty acts that you are about to do. Maybe they are not so big in terms of history, but they are mighty acts in your own life. The epiphanies in your own life. I think that is what a lot of psalms are about.

> The LORD is my shepherd, I shall not want;
>> he makes me lie down in green pastures.
> He leads me beside still waters;
>> he restores my soul. . . .
> Even though I walk through the valley of the shadow
> of death . . .
>
> PSALM 23:1–4

The Psalmist is talking about moments when it was as if the Lord had led him into green pastures. When he did indeed walk through the valley of the shadow of death, there was a sense of the presence of God, nonetheless, that kept him from being afraid. The Psalms are directing us to those moments in our own lives. Don't neglect those moments. Don't miss those moments when God speaks to you, as he did in a funny way to me through the bird in song this morning, as he does to all of us, in all sorts of ways, and all of the time.

■ ■ ■

And then, of course, the New Testament tells us to stop, look, and listen again. I think of Jesus, and I think of Emily Dickinson, of all people, who said a wonderful thing in a letter she wrote: "You know, there is only one commandment I have never broken"—which is wonderful, for I can't imagine Emily Dickinson breaking any commandments, though I'm certain she has broken as many as the rest of us—"and that is the commandment, 'Consider the lilies of the field.'" Wonderful. She is referring, of course, to what Jesus says to the crowd on the hillside—"Consider the lilies of the field, how they grow; they neither toil nor spin; yet I tell you, even Solomon in all his glory was not arrayed like one of these" (Matthew 6:28–29 RSV).

It's a joke, in a way, the thought of commandments like this, but in another way it is the kind of commandment that it seems to me Jesus gives in different ways again and again, that this life is, in a way, a parable: Consider the lilies of the field. Consider what it was to find that thing you had lost, that coin, that ring your mother gave you, that photograph that could not be replaced and suddenly it is there. Consider your heart itself . . . consider that. Consider the lost sheep. Consider the dead sparrow. Consider the way leaven works in bread. Consider the way the seeds grow, that tiny little bit of a seed that grows and grows and grows until it's a tree as big as Texas. Pay attention to these things.

And, of course, Jesus says that the greatest commandment is this: loving God and loving our neighbors. I don't know what it means to love God—really, I'm not all that good at it—but I think one of the things it means is, just as in the case of loving anybody else, you stop and watch and wait. *Listen for God*, stop and watch and wait for him. To love God means to *pay attention*, be mindful, be open to the possibility that God is with you in ways that, unless you have your eyes open, you may never glimpse. He speaks words that, unless you have your ears open, you may never hear. Draw near to him as best you can.

One Christmas Eve in Vermont when my children were small, we did the things you do when your children are small on Christmas Eve. We stuffed and hung their stockings. We put out a draught of cider and a cookie on the mantelpiece for Santa Claus—who would be tired by the time he got there through all that snow—and we put them to bed and then went upstairs and got the presents out of the closet off the guest room, and we dragged them down and put them under the Christmas tree. Somebody at some time had given me Charles Dickens's recipe for wassail, and I said, "Well, I've never tasted wassail. Let's make it." It's a hideous mixture of beer and sherry and toast. But I made it, we drank it, and it was awful, and then we were just about to tumble exhausted into bed when I remembered that our neighbor just a short distance down the hill had gone off to Florida, I think, for a couple of weeks and had asked me if I would feed his sheep while he was gone. Late as it was, I knew I had to do it. So my brother and I put on our boots and our coats, and we trudged down the hill through a lot of snow to the barn where we each picked up a couple of bales of hay and carried them out to the sheep shed in the back and pulled the string on the 40-watt bulb, and the sheep came bumbling around the way sheep do, and we split the strings of the bales and shook the dust out and put them in the rack. And there was the smell of the hay and the bumbling of the sheep and the dim light and the snow falling outside and it was Christmas Eve, and only then did I realize where I was. Being a minister trained me to notice things, but it was only then that

I noticed the manger, though I might have not noticed it at all. And it seems to me the world is a manger, the whole bloody mess of it, where God is being born again and again and again and again and again and again. You've got your mind on so many other things. You are so busy with this and that, you don't see it. You don't notice it.

■ ■ ■

There's one other anecdote that illuminates this somehow. My wife, Judy, and our youngest daughter, Sharman, and I went to SeaWorld in San Antonio one day. It's one of those great big aquatic jamborees, full of hoopla and hokum, and T-shirts and loud music and frozen bananas dipped in chocolate and all that, but don't knock it because the main attraction is something that everybody should see. Well, the main attraction, I am sure you know, is you sit in the stands and there before you is a huge tank of crystal clear, turquoise-colored water in front of a big platform on which stand these beautiful young women and handsome young men in bathing suits, and then at a signal, out come these creatures of such beauty. There is no describing them. They call them killer whales. (Why killer? I wonder what they call us . . .) These great big creatures are cousins of ours, these mammals of pearl gray, indescribably beautiful that swim at enormous rates through crystal clear water and jump through hoops that the young people hold for them, and the sun shines and the sky is blue and it is just unbelievable. As I watched it, I found tears streaking down my cheeks, and ah!—I was embarrassed by them. I'm a neurotic man a hundred ways to Sunday, but I thought, here I am crying at this marvelous thing. And I turned to my wife and daughter and they also had tears in their eyes. We were crying because we caught a glimpse of the peace of God when man and beast and sun and water and hope were all somehow dancing together in this wonderful dance. We caught a glimpse of Eden, of the way things were supposed to be.

So loving God means, as Jesus says, consider the lilies of the field. Consider SeaWorld. Consider feeding your neighbor's sheep on Christmas Eve and loving each other. Jesus says, Love the Lord thy God with thy heart and soul and strength, and also your neighbor. And that is the same thing.

■ ■ ■

To love your neighbor is to see your neighbor. To see somebody, really to see somebody, you have to love somebody. You have to see people the way Rembrandt saw the old lady, not just a face that comes at you the way a dry leaf blows at you down the path like all other dry leaves, but in a way that you realize the face is something the likes of which you have never seen before and will never see again. To love somebody we must see that person's face, and once in a while we do. Usually it is because something jolts us into seeing it.

The faces we lose track of most easily are the faces of the people who are closest to us, the people we love the most whose faces we see so often that we can't really see them anymore. There's Judy. There's Sharman. There's George. There's Mary. We name them as we name the fog, they become just words, we name them out of existence, and that's it. Imagine.

I preached all one winter long at a church in Manchester, a Baptist church, the minister of which had left and they hadn't gotten a new one. My job was supposed to be just preaching, the pastoring part, and all of the other things that go on in churches was done by other people. One day I was shaking hands like my old friend George Buttrick used to after the sermon and saying the usual amenities, exchanging that how-do-you-do, when one old woman came out of that church whom I had never noticed before. Sallow, hollow-chested, grim looking, and I said, "How are you?"—dumb question—and she said, "I'm just as well as can be expected." I'll always remember those words. They were not the expected words, and somehow those words made me afraid. I could not help but fear for her faith, and even though my arrangement was not to do anything but preach, I thought I can't not go see somebody who says, merely, *I'm as well as can be expected.*

So I went to see her, and I dreaded it because I thought there would be tears and it would last too long and she would tell me all of her troubles and I wouldn't know what to say. I wouldn't be able to help her. What can you do for a lonely old woman? But none of those things happened. Instead I fell in love with that old woman, and I went to see her, not for her sake but for my sake, year after year for about seven years until one St. Valentine's Day she died. My life was enriched by her. I experienced love and I was able to love her too, all because I happened to see her face by grace. By grace. I didn't think, "I'm a minister. I'm supposed to be good to people." I didn't—no such thought as that. Quite the reverse. I wanted to distance myself from anybody whose need I thought was answerable by me, but I couldn't help myself. So sometimes we see them, sometimes we hear them. I heard her as she spoke. But to love means to look and to listen, listen to the sounds of your life, and sometimes we do and sometimes we don't. Sometimes we don't see people because we choose damn well not to see them.

I remember another incident where I went to the office of a man who had a job at a printing business. I had some printing to do, of course, but also I knew lots of things about him. He was having trouble with his marriage. He was having trouble with alcohol. He was having trouble with his business. His whole life was falling apart, and again it's funny the question we always ask each other—*How are you?* What more human question is there than *How are you?* but whoever expects an answer? It's not supposed to have an answer. And I said to this fellow when I went into his office, "How are you?" knowing, of course, how he was. And there was what seemed to me an almost unbearable moment, a series of moments, when he didn't answer. And I thought to myself, *My God! He's going to tell me!*

Well, he laughed, but why were we laughing at that? Because if he told me how he was—which was dying, really— what would there be for me to do but to try to somehow lift him up? I dreaded it. To my infinite relief, after a moment he said, "I'm fine. How are you?" and we went on with the business of the day.

So we are told to love. We are told to listen. We are told to look. But a lot of the time we don't because we choose damn well not to, and because only a saint could do it all the time, I think. You have to choose who to listen to because if you listen to *everybody* and you look at *everybody*—seeing *every* face the way Rembrandt saw that woman's face—how could you make it down half a city block? You couldn't. If you listened to what *everybody* says to you, how could you survive a day? But we can do more than we do—more than we do, surely we could do that.

■ ■ ■

To look with the imagination as well as with the eyes. To look with empathy and compassion. To see each other as Rembrandt saw the old woman, as Holden Caulfield and Seymour Glass with X-ray eyes, which, of course, Jesus supremely has. The most precious words from his lips—and to me I think the most precious of all—are, "Come unto me all ye who labor and are heavy laden, and I will refresh you." Those words are addressed not only to the people who are obviously laboring and heavy laden—the people in nursing homes, the poor, the dispossessed, the starving—they are addressed to everybody. They are addressed to the beautiful girl on her wedding day. They are addressed to the man who just made a million dollars. They are addressed to the young graduate of whatever it is, who is heading off into the great big world. Jesus sees that all of us labor and are heavy laden and are in need of rest or are in need of him or in need of peace. So we are to see each other like that, as Jesus sees us, framed as if each one of our faces is seen by him. And the frame he sees us in, if you have to give it a word, is the frame of love. He sees us because he loves us; he loves us because he sees us.

Imagine yourself in a big city in a crowd of people. What it would be like to see all the people in the crowd like Jesus does—an anonymous crowd with old ones and young ones, fat ones and thin ones, attractive ones and ugly ones—think what it would be like to love them. If our faith is true, if there is a God, and if God loves, he loves each one of those. Try to see them as loved. And then try to see them, these faces, as loved by you. What would it be like to love these people, to love these faces—the lovable faces, the kind faces, gentle, compassionate faces? That's not so hard. But there are lots of other faces—disagreeable faces, frightening faces, frightened faces, cruel faces, closed faces. I find if you think of them as your family, it helps. You can do it, and it's an exercise worth trying.

What it would be like to love each one of these faces, to see the face and to love the face for what lies there, to meet the face that is finally—as that minister said in answer to C. S. Lewis's question "What did Hitler look like?"—"Like Christ."

Ah, they are all peculiar treasures. I used that as a title of a book—it's from Exodus where God said to Israel, "You shall be a peculiar treasure unto me above all people." God meant it for all of us. And when I think of God treasuring us, I often think of another art that I haven't talked about yet—about television. I think of television as an art—abused and used for all the wrong purposes, and corny and dreadful in lots of ways, but in some cases enormously powerful. Like that old sitcom *All in the Family*, for instance—Archie Bunker and Meathead and Gloria and all that. It makes you laugh a lot, but it's also moving, rather like Garrison Keillor who has the same great gift for being very funny and at the same time very moving. I remember one scene in particular where Meathead, Archie's son-in-law, and Gloria, Archie's daughter, were leaving for the West Coast, and this was the good-bye scene. Archie and Meathead were standing out on the front stoop of that little house where they lived and where Archie and Meathead had fought all those years. Archie is an arch-bigot, a racist, a sexist, and more, while Meathead is a fire-breathing liberal, and they've been tangling for years and years and years. Now here they were about to say good-bye to each other and speechless. Neither could think of a thing to say. All of a sudden, Meathead threw his arms around Archie Bunker and said, "You thought I hated you, but all the time I loved you." An incandescent moment. And Archie's face sort of folded in, like it was just punched with a fist. He had no words to say, but it was as if he spoke those words too—you thought I hated you, you thought I was indifferent to you, you thought

I wasn't around, you thought I didn't exist . . . but all the time, I loved you.

Love each other like that. Love each other knowing that you are loved. Love yourself knowing that I love you.

■ ■ ■

The deepest mystery of all, I think, is the one to which biblical faith points, which is the idea that we are made not only of matter that comes from the earth and stars, but we are made in the image of God. Whatever that means. I don't know what that means altogether, but I think it means that we bear his mark upon us. Deep within us. The face of Christ is within us, his thumbprint is upon us. The world adds all sorts of things to that holy self that God made, but it still is there, and though we lose track of it in a million ways, I think it remains, if we are lucky at all, as a source of goodness, of flashes of insight, good dreams, good prayers that somehow pray themselves, of healing.

I think that is the place from which all true art comes, and by true art I mean art that doesn't just entertain—perfectly all right to do that—but true art that nourishes the spirit, that illuminates the mind, that deepens the understanding, that deepens our humanity. I think that what true art, and true religion, does at its best is to put each one of us in touch with that holy part of ourselves, with that source from which art and love comes, and from which all good, wise things come, so that we—by virtue of this painting, this poem, this ballet, this piece of music, this Scripture—become finally, truly, human at last.

PART 2

LISTENING
FOR GOD IN THE
STORIES
WE TELL

CHAPTER 3

THE
LAUGHING ROOM
OF MAYA
ANGELOU

I first met Maya Angelou when the Trinity Institute brought us together to speak for a series of lectures. The Institute does this every year, and the lectures are frankly geared for burned-out Episcopal clergy—men and women who simply have had it. They think what these clergy people need is a kind of shot in the arm to keep them going for the next lap, and what they've mostly done is to give them pretty much an academic shot in the arm. They've had some very fancy people indeed—the theologian Jürgen Moltmann, Bishop Tutu, the archbishop of Canterbury, and all sorts of folk like that talking about what you'd imagine they would talk about—ethics, and the church, and the role of Christianity in terms of race, and so on. I really don't know why they came to me. I cannot explain that, but they did, and this awfully nice Episcopal priest asked if I would give a series of lectures on the subject of story. That's the big fad in theology, and when I hear it, it just drives me mad. So I said, "Certainly not. I have no interest in doing that at all." My brother Jamie happened to be sitting in the room where I was having this phone conversation, and when I hung up he said, "I think you must've had that poor man in tears," because I had so many negative things to say about fads and I was sick of story and I didn't want to talk about it or think about it or hear about it.

But during our conversation, this Episcopal fellow said, "Well, could I come down and see you anyway?" I was in Florida at the time and he was in New York, and I figured if anybody was willing to come that far to talk about such a thing, I would certainly let him come. So he came, and he said that he had thought of what I had told him and had dropped the notion he had originally presented to me, but he wondered if I would be interested in simply coming and talking about my own story. Of course, I had recently published two books at that time, one of them called *The Sacred Journey* and one of them called *Now and Then*, in which I set about to relate a sort of spiritual autobiography in the sense that I simply looked back on my life from its very beginning to listen to moments when I thought God had spoken to me. I think that's the most fascinating story anybody can tell, especially anybody who happens to be religiously inclined—How did you get to be the way you are when there are a million reasons for not being that way at all? How did *you* happen? So that's what I had done in these two earlier books, and this fellow asked would I be willing to do it again, and that was just the right question to ask me because I'd been sort of thinking about doing that sort of thing anyway and here was a chance to do it for them. So I agreed to it.

They always have two people giving these lectures, and the other person they got was this extraordinary woman named Maya Angelou, who has told her story in not two but I think something like five volumes, the first of which is a marvelous book called *I Know Why the Caged Bird Sings*.

Maya Angelou is a large woman about my height, black, beautiful, and so full of energy you can warm your hands in front of her. She was born in the South and brought up in great poverty by her grandmother in the little town of Stamps, Arkansas. Awful things happened to her. She was raped at the age of eight, not a violent rape but a sort of one-thing-leads-to-another rape by a boyfriend of her mother whom she'd gone to visit. She came back from that experience afraid to tell anybody about it, but she eventually told her little brother Bailey that this thing had happened. By a fluke, within a couple of days of that, word came that the man who'd raped her had died, and she was terrified that her words had killed him. So she was mute for five years—didn't say anything for five years. Well, she grew up, became a dancer, became a waitress, became a cook, and for a brief time she was a prostitute. She fell on evil times—the man whom she was with at that time said he needed some money and, if she wouldn't mind, could she entertain some of his friends, and she did that for a time. Then she started to write and one thing led to another—acclaimed books, operas, films, and TV shows. She's a Renaissance woman, in other words. Full of life, full of beans, full of stories. And I just want to tell you a couple of things she said that moved me.

One thing she said was that every once in a while as she moved around the world she would meet somebody who would say with considerable pride, "I'm a Christian." And whenever she heard that she would say, "I try very hard to be a Christian. It's very difficult for me to be a Christian. I work at it. A lot of things are working against it in me, though." But what she was really thinking when she would hear someone say, "I'm a

Christian," is, "Already?" It's a good thing to remember. Already a Christian . . . Wow.

Another thing she said that I loved was that on certain plantations during slavery days there was a rule against laughter amongst slaves. Slaves were not supposed to laugh, which is fascinating. I never heard that before, but I can see why there might've been such a rule. If you're enslaving somebody, you don't want them laughing, do you? It's harder to make a slave out of a laughing person. The danger I suppose always is they might laugh at you, they might laugh at slavery, who knows. But she said the slaves could not live without laughing, so they devised something which they called the laughter barrel. They kept a barrel somewhere and when the impulse to laugh became overpowering they would simply lean into it, as if to get something out of the barrel, and let it all go. It's a wonderful picture.

Then she recalled for everyone the really marvelous high church Episcopal service that took place before our lectures began—there was incense and there was chanting and there were vestments—and Maya said, "I just looked at that service, and you Episcopalians do it so well. Those gorgeous vestments you wear and those candles and the singing. And there was that man who came in holding that great silver cross with this look of great serenity on his face. And I thought to myself, what you should have right off the vestry is a *laughter room*. You parade around with all these wonderful things, and every once in a while you go in there and *ha ha ha!*, and then you come out of the laughter room and you pick up the cross and keep going."

The wonderful truth of that, of course, is we act in these religious traditions and rituals as if we know what we're doing. None of us knows. We all think a church service is when you sing this here, then you pray that there, and you read this here, and you stand here and you stand there, as if this is the appropriate, natural way to worship him who is beyond our wildest dreams, whose glory we can in no sense capture in any kind of ecclesiastical box. What marvelous advice Maya gave us that we might well do with in our own rituals, our own pieties, our own way of doing things—to stop for a moment and just *ha ha ha!* And God very likely is doing the same thing.

The most moving part of my time at Trinity happened after one of Maya's lectures. There had been a number of questions and one person asked her a question about racism—has it gotten better, has it gotten worse, is it better in one place in the West Coast than the East Coast? And she had said, "Let me tell you a story." She said she had been in the San Francisco Bay area fifteen years or so before to do a public television program on African art, and out of the blue one day she got a telephone call from a white man who told her that he had a collection of a certain kind of African statue and perhaps she would like to come over and look at them. So she went over and they were wonderful examples of whatever form of African art they were, and he lent them to her and she used them in ways that pleased him. Through this experience, they became great friends. She went to his house for dinner a number of times, got to know his wife, and Maya had them over to her place for dinner, and they were terrific pals. She said it had been one of the bright spots during her time there, and then the public television show was over and she went back to wherever it was she went. Time went by and about four or five years later she returned to the Bay Area, this time for a longer period of time. So right away she called up her friend, who told her he'd be delighted to see her again. He said, "Let me just catch you up on what I've been doing since I saw you last. I have been in Europe working on the problem with American troops over there. It's not an easy row for them to hoe in a way," he said, "and it's especially hard for the black troops for obvious reasons. There aren't too many blacks over there, but *our* boys are also having a hard—"

She interrupted him. "What did you say?"

"I said, in Europe it's especially hard for the black troops, and that our boys are also—"

"What did you say?" She had interrupted him again, she told us, because she wanted him to hear it.

So again, "Well, the black troops . . ." and then he got it. "Oh my God! What have I said to you, of all people? The black troops . . . our boys. I'm so embarrassed I simply have to stop talking. I'm going to hang up. To say this to you, of all people."

And Maya had said, "No, don't. Don't hang up. This is just the time we need to talk. This is what racism is beneath the level of liberal utterance and superficial friendship, the sort of deeply rooted sense of *we* and *they*, the whites, the blacks, the browns, the whatever it is."

So they finished off their conversation agreeing that they would meet. Then she said after that she had tried to call him innumerable times and left messages of one kind or another, and there was never any response at all.

She told us that was the end, and when she had finished that question and answer time, she had been obviously very moved and sort of shaken by it. The next day she had started her lecture reflecting on this story about racism, saying, "As I left the room yesterday, a man stood up and said, 'Here I am!'"

No sooner had these words left her lips when this small, bearded, white Episcopal clergyman suddenly stood up in our midst a few rows behind me and walked down the aisle, up onto the platform, and put his arms around her. He was, of course, her friend who had been too embarrassed to talk to her anymore. And she cried and he cried and all of us cried because we just got a glimpse of the kingdom of God. So moving. So gorgeous.

The other thing Maya Angelou said that moved me was when the two of us were being introduced by the friendly fellow I had made cry on the phone. I had given my lecture first, which was based, as I said, on my spiritual autobiography, and after I was done, this fellow introduced Maya, saying, "Ms. Angelou will now get up and tell you her story, and it will be a very different story from the one that you have just heard from Frederick Buechner." As he said that, Maya Angelou, who was sitting in the front row and shaking her head from side to side, got up, and she said he was wrong. She said, "I have exactly the same story to tell as Frederick Buechner." I was very touched by that because in so many ways, what stories could be more different? I'm a man and she's a woman, I'm white, she's black, she grew up in dire poverty while by comparison I grew up with riches, though God knows we weren't rich, and yet she said it's the same story. And what she meant I think is that at a certain level we do, all of us, with all the differences, we do all have the same story. When it comes to the business of how do you become a human being, how do you manage to believe, how do you have faith in a world that gives you 14,000 reasons every week not to believe, how do you survive—especially surviving our own childhoods as Maya Angelou survived hers and we've all survived ours—at that level we all have the same story, and therefore anybody's story can illuminate our own.

And that's the only reason I have, the only justification, to tell you my story. Who gives a hoot about my story? But you can give a hoot about it because also it's in many ways your story.

CHAPTER 4

THE SUBTERRANEAN GRACE OF GOD, OR WHY STORIES MATTER

I woke up this morning for some reason thinking about that wonderful eleventh chapter of the Epistle to the Hebrews, which says,

> Now faith is the assurance of things hoped for, the conviction of things not seen. For by it the men of old received divine approval. By faith we understand that the world was created by the word of God, so that what is seen was made out of things which do not appear. (Hebrews 11:1–3, RSV)

Then there's that wonderful catalogue of the heroes of the faith: by faith Abel offered to God a more acceptable sacrifice than Cain . . . by faith Enoch was taken up so that he should not see death . . . by faith Abraham obeyed when he was called to go out to a place that he was to receive as an inheritance . . . by faith Sarah . . . by faith Isaac . . . and so on. These all died in faith, not having "received what was promised," but having seen it and greeted it from afar, and having acknowledged that they were strangers in exile on the earth, for people who speak thus make it clear that they are seeking a homeland. Wonderful passage.

And I thought of little Dorothy Gale from Kansas, who was in Oz to find the wizard, hoping he'd find a way of sending her home, and that in a sense we are all looking for home, a place that we glimpsed only from afar, but we have glimpsed it. And I thought also of the church as an outpost of home, as a threshold over which we see a little of what maybe home will be like.

And then I thought of all the nasty things I sometimes say about church, and I say them because of my experience where I happen to live in New England where for me at least the churches have just not come through. I've gone hungering and I haven't been fed. But recently I was giving a series of lectures in the southern part of the country with a man named John Huffman, and I listened to what he said with great interest, but maybe more than that, I watched him and listened to him as a human being. And I thought if I were lucky enough to live in a part of the world where I had as my pastor someone as wise and compassionate and committed as I sensed him to be, maybe I would have a different view of what church is all about. I loved what he said about giving all that you know and all you don't know about yourself to all you know and all you don't know about God. That's a wonderful way to say it.

It's difficult to help people see that the Bible isn't really a book of moral platitudes, full of plaster saints and moral exemplars and boringness, as the rather dreary format of the Bible and also the dreary way in which it is presented so often suggests. It's difficult to speak of holy things through the traditional language of doctrine and the language of biblical faith, trying to re-animate it, trying to get people interested in it, trying to see that it's not quite as bankrupt as they had been led to believe, very often led to believe by people who themselves loved it but weren't very good at conveying it. And that is certainly one of the languages in which we speak about religion—the formal religious language.

But the trouble is, of course, that for many people the language of doctrine, the language of Zion, the religious words, the biblical categories and so on are like coins that have been handled so long that the images rub off. You don't know what they are, you can't read them anymore, they're rubbed smooth. You don't know what they're worth. You've heard these words, and you've heard them, and heard them, and heard them to the point where they lose their currency. They don't have the power they once did. So don't be surprised if you find yourself asking, Isn't there some new language for speaking of holy things? Of course there is, and there are also nonverbal ways. Like when Maya Angelou stood on the stage after her lecture, and out of the audience rose up that little bearded white Episcopal priest who walked up on the stage and embraced her, and she him, and everybody wept in that room. What more wonderful language could you find than that nonverbal language to express a great deal of what we mean about almost everything—love and the kingdom of God and so on.

What I tried to suggest in the first chapter of this book is that art is such a language, and I don't mean just the arts that involve words, but the nonverbal arts like music and painting. You can hardly go to a great concert, as I did this spring with Judy to the Bach festival in Bethlehem, Pennsylvania, and hear that music without hearing profundities about the mystery of God and the mystery of human beings conveyed through the music. It's the same way with great paintings, like when we went to that Monet exhibit—the grace that is somehow conveyed by the haystack and all of those different kinds of light and dimness and rain.

■ ■ ■

So there are these ways of speaking about holy things, and then of course there also is the art of writing, particularly stories, which is the one that I dabbled in, using a story to convey what faith is. Of course of all of the arts, none I think is more basic to the nature of biblical faith than the art of storytelling, because if you think about it that is basically what the Bible is. It is a series of stories, whether they're stories like the ones in Genesis, or whether they're the narrative of Israel's history, or the Gospels themselves. They all are recounting things that happened, or that could have happened, or that were imagined to have happened in ways that convey a depth of truth that could not perhaps be conveyed in any other way. Think about Jesus himself who said nothing to his disciples without a parable, nothing. It's fascinating, think about that. In other words he didn't teach the way anybody today does, the way Paul Tillich taught or the way John Huffman and I have been trying to teach, or the way any theologian or preacher is apt to teach. He taught simply by telling these very commonplace, very simple stories.

The creed is the same way, when you think of it. We don't believe in a lot of doctrinal *statements*—I believe in God the father who made heaven and earth, Jesus Christ who was conceived of the Holy Ghost, born of the Virgin Mary, who suffered under Pontius Pilate, was crucified, died and was buried, descended into hell and on the third day he rose again from the dead, and that and this . . . No, I believe that these things *happened*, this series of events *happened*. You don't say I believe in predestination, I believe in the blood atonement, I believe in the priesthood of all believers. You say I believe that this *happened*—he was born, he did this, he did that, this happened to him, and then this happened to him and that happened to him and so on.

So stories are basic to the faith in that sense, and certainly they are basic to the faith of all of us, because I think our faith, if it's worth anything, comes from the story that each one of us has lived in this world, not just from what we heard from the pulpit. Our faith comes from our own individual stories. It is through our stories that God speaks to us and gives us the sense that they have a plot. E. M. Forster, that wonderful English novelist and short story writer of the earlier part of the twentieth century, described the distinction between a story and a plot like this: A story is to say the king died and then the queen died. That's just a sequence, a chronological sequence of events. This happened and that happened and then that happened. But a plot is, the king died and then the queen died of grief. In other words, plot suggests a because, a cause and effect, a shape, a getting to someplace—when the king died the queen died because she loved the king.

I think that a part of what to tell one's own story in a religious sense means is to affirm that there is a plot to one's life. It's not just incident following incident without any particular direction or purpose, but things are happening in order to take you somewhere. Just the way a story begins and has a middle and an end. Things are somehow wrapped up at the end, and everything in some fashion can be seen to have led to this inevitable conclusion and to have had its own place, however circumstantial and odd and out-of-the-way some of those things that happened may have been. They had their purpose in the overall shape and texture and reality of one's story.

That certainly is what I discovered when I wrote those autobiographical books looking back at my life and finding that very often things that seemed at the time to have had very little significance were key points in the plot of my life. I can see myself at eleven or twelve in Bermuda as vividly as I see the line of trees out my window now, wheeling my bicycle up the little dirt path on one of the hills, and down toward me comes an Anglican priest dressed the way they did in the day of Laurence Sterne with gaiters and a black coat and a broad brim flat hat through the golden dust and the green palm leaves and the coral walls. It was a moment I've never forgotten because it was part of the plot of my life. I remember it because it was a clue to what my whole life and faith is all about.

I think of when that poor man called me up in Florida to invite me to speak about story for the Trinity lectures, and my gorge rose and I said those terrible things to him. I remember the reason I said those things is because story's become such a fad, and I still have a horrible feeling that what story means to some people is the minister gets up and tries to convey his message by usually telling a perfectly wretched story. I remember listening to one man who was famous for story sermons, and I sat through this awful thing where he took the story of the prodigal son and recast it as a Western. Jesus tells that story so beautifully—it's so suggestive and nothing is spelled out, but every point this story-pastor made had been contrived and thought out, and every word of dialogue was . . . well I almost was sick, and at the end of it he said *Amen*, and I thought *Oh, God, forgive him for he knows not what he's doing.*

■ ■ ■

But there are only two stories that make any difference—God's story and the human story. We all are living out different versions of those two stories with an infinite number of variations. God's story, or the story of God and man, is simple—God made the world and loved the world, the world got lost, and God has spent the rest of human history trying somehow to bring the world back to himself. That is the story of God and man as I think each one of us has experienced it. It's really as simple as that and as complex as that.

And man's story, as when Maya Angelou said her story is exactly the same as my story, is that we are all born in the same way, we all have to somehow survive our childhoods—the bad parts of them, the confusing and painful parts of them—we all have to find a self to be, we all grow old and grow sick and finally die. This is the human story. And in the process of living out that story, God's story intersects with ours. He appears in our stories. In that sense, to talk about story actually fascinates me, and if that poor man had invited me to come and do that from the first, I would have leapt at the chance, and in fact it's what in a way I ended up doing for him—telling as much of my story as seemed relevant to the way in which those two stories, God's story and man's story, intermesh.

As a writer also of stories besides my own, I've tried to do just that, to present the stories of human beings as honestly as I can—people who are born as we are into the world, who are just as messed up by it and screwed up by it as the rest of us, and have all sorts of adventures the way we all have adventures, and yet who are touched here and there by the presence of God in all sorts of unexpected ways, and often in ways that the people who are touched by God might not identify as Godly ways . . . they don't know it's God, necessarily, but it is.

I think it was François Mauriac, the French Catholic novelist, who said of Graham Greene that he, in his books, dealt with a subterranean presence of grace. That's a wonderful way to put it. It's beneath the surface; it's not right there like the brass band announcing itself, but it comes and it touches and it strikes in ways that always leave us free to either not even notice it or to notice it and draw back from it, because life is complicated enough, and if God is somehow put into the complexity of it, it becomes more complicated, so we just look the other way. Like those people in *Candid Camera* who, when fantastic, miraculous things happen, look the other way because it is just too disturbing. It's hard enough to get through a day without believing that a car can drive down the street with no driver. It's hard enough to get through life without thinking there is really a God who is here moving among us to take us somewhere.

But that's what I try to do, to speak about human beings and the rough-and-tumble of human existence, human beings who are here and there touched by grace through people they come to know or through things that happen to them or things that don't happen to them. All of the books and authors that I most deeply admire do that. Like Flannery O'Connor—all of her stories are about grace happening. Or Graham Greene's *The Power and the Glory*, the novel that of all novels for me has had the greatest effect—through this seedy little half-baked, cowardly, adulterous Catholic priest who somehow by the grace of God is kept alive in revolutionary Mexico and how every life he touches is somehow brought a little bit more to life by his presence, making him a saint in a way, not a saint in the sense of a plaster saint, of a haloed saint, but a saint in the sense of a person as mixed up as the rest of us through whom, nonetheless, God's grace was able to work. This priest became a means of grace.

■ ■ ■

I write very much the way I dream, with the same mystery. Just as you go to sleep at night and up out of the depths of who you are this dream comes, so in a certain state of mind, whatever that is, out of the depths of you comes a character or two or three and a situation and a place and a feeling. It's a sort of given-ness of the book, like the given-ness of a dream. Unbidden it comes. You can't force it, and you're very lucky if it does come because it doesn't always. You can think of a dream as your own creation, nobody else dreamed it, you dreamed it. It comes out of the depths of who you are, your subconscious, out of all the things that happened during the day, the raw material, and you dream about something somebody said, but why *that* something? There's a sense in which the dream is yours, your creation, yet at the same time as everybody knows, the dream speaks to you a word that seems to come from someplace other than yourself, because it's often a revelation. Everybody's had dreams that almost wake them up with their truth. So it's both a word *from* you, but it's also a word *to* you. I think everybody could name dreams like that. I've written about several of mine, and I'll tell you of one—if you've read my books you'll know it, but I'll tell it anyway because it's one of the truest dreams I've dreamed, about being in a hotel.

I used to dream a lot about being in hotels, whatever that means. I had this wonderful room that I remembered less visually than about how good I felt in that room. It was just the right place for me. I felt at peace and happy. And then the dream went on and I had other adventures which I've forgotten. But I found myself back in the hotel again trying to find that room where I felt so good, so at peace, but unfortunately I didn't remember what the room number was. It was a big hotel. So I went down to the desk and somebody at the desk was there, and I said I was trying to find this room but I can't remember the number. He said, "Oh, it's very easy to get to that room any time that you want. It doesn't have a number, it has a name." I said, "What is the name of that room?" He said, "The name of that room is Remember." It woke me up, in more ways than one. I don't understand entirely what it meant, but it somehow gave me a clue. It gives us all a clue that to remember far enough, to remember deeply enough, is to remember God, it's to remember Eden, to remember where you came from, and that through remembering you work your way back to some truth that is a liberating and healing truth. It's been true of me thinking back through those moments when God spoke to me. It's been true for me when I was in therapy, that whole healing process of remembering, real remembering with somebody to help you remember, to confront again, to relive old shadows, which somehow dispels them.

■ ■ ■

I wrote a series of four novels about a man named Leo Bebb who for me was a saint. How Bebb came about is an interesting story. I went to a barbershop, and I was waiting my turn and there was a copy of *Life* magazine, which I opened, and an earlier customer's hair was sort of stuck in the crack of the magazine at a story about a religious con man whose name I will not mention here. I'm always afraid maybe he is still around or some of his heirs are, and they will sue me for libel. But there he was, he had done time for indecent exposure, and he had cashed bad checks, and he ran a little sort of weird flat-roofed church in Florida somewhere. There was a picture of him, a man with a great glittering rack of false teeth, and the magazine told just enough about him that it somehow triggered something in me, and up out of the depths of who I am arose a whole world about which I didn't really know anything. I knew Florida a little bit because I had spent a few weeks each winter for four or five years down there, but I had never known a man like Leo Bebb, as I called him. I had never had any dealings with a church like this, but it came up out of me from the same place that dreams come.

As I've said, a dream is both yours, your creation, yet also somehow comes from afar, speaks to you in something other than your own tongue. It certainly was true of Leo Bebb. I dreamed him, I thought up his name, I based his looks on this picture in *Life* magazine and a few other things. Just like the way a dream makes use of the raw material of the day before, you know you dream about somebody you saw or something you heard, Leo Bebb emerged for me that way. I remember there was a man at Exeter with a fat face and an H for a mouth, sort of straight across and two little hinges. A wonderful man full of fun. Then I remember there was a marvelous ad on television for garters or something like that. I think it must've been for men's garters because there was a wonderful sort of fat man with a pair of socks and garters and just his underpants, and he danced around to show that the garters wouldn't drop off of his feet, and while he danced he had one eyelid that would go up and down once in a while, sort of a droopy eyelid, and then it would come back up again. Well, those two men combined to become Bebb's face. In other words out of all of these little things, I dreamed up this character of Bebb and made him out of bits and pieces of what I'd seen and so on. But then Bebb took on a life of his own. I had thought of him, he was a religious con man like the man in *Life* magazine. He had also done five years in a federal penitentiary for indecent exposure before children. He ran a religious diploma mill, ordaining people through the mail—you would send in your money and he would send you a diploma. He had all sorts of reprehensible things about him, and there was a young man who went down to investigate him. And as I wrote the book, what the young man discovered was that the reprehensible things were only part of the truth about Leo Bebb. Yes, he was a religious con man, but he also was a saint. He was a life-giver. He brought people to life. He was good company. He was full of something so rich and alive that you couldn't be with him without somehow becoming a little bit richer and more alive yourself.

And what happened was, that happened to me—Leo Bebb in a funny way brought me to life. I had sort of written myself into a dead end street as a novelist. The novel before this one was called *The Entrance to Porlock*, which I suspect few, if any, have read. It was a sort of strangled book. I did the best I could and I took great care with the language, but it somehow brought me to the end of a valley that comes down, no place to go from there, and I was sort of treading water. All of a sudden along came this ebullient, crooked, wild, crazy, life-giving Southern man and he brought me to life. He allowed me for the first time to be funny in books, to let people say outrageous things and do outrageous things. It was a wonderful dream. And it brought me to life, it really did. It gave me a whole new chapter of my life, not just as a writer but almost as a human being.

Leo Bebb, who had done time for indecent exposure, became a symbol to me because he exposed himself in more ways than that. He was marvelously there, all of him, the good with the bad. He didn't try to hide it. He couldn't hide it. He just came out with what came into his head, and that somehow encouraged me to do the same. I was brought up in New England where one doesn't speak easily about oneself, but it was out of that somehow that grew the autobiographical books where I was willing to expose to the world some of my secrets. And I learned so much from my own creation that one could say I became partly Leo Bebb's creation. I mean, from him I learned to expose myself—not as he had, I never ended up in jail—but to tell the truth about myself, to my readers and also, importantly, to myself. And in the telling of my variation of the human story, I discovered cracks in the ground of my life through which I was able to glimpse the subterranean, life-giving grace of God.

PART 3

TELLING THE TRUTH

CHAPTER 5

A LONG
WAY TO GO

The twentieth century comprised three worlds. There was the world before the Second World War, which nobody who didn't live there, I think, can even imagine—there was a kind of innocence abroad, where this country was somehow unquestionably a great country, a powerful and rich country. Then there was the Second World War—if ever there's been a war between the forces of light and the forces of darkness, it seemed to be that one. There was in that world a kind of hopefulness and a kind of innocence, which is the best word I can give it. Then the war ended and lots of terrible things happened. The Cold War happened—cold as death, terrifying, the possibility of annihilation, the atomic bomb. And then with the coming down of the Berlin Wall and the collapse of the Soviet Union this new world emerged—whatever in heaven's name it will become—with wonderful possibilities for good, sort of steering in the direction of tolerance, sanity, and concern for the environment, and yet terrible, terrible possibilities for ill. Our own nation, as I see it, is really coming apart at the seams in countless ways, a sort of outgrowth of nationalism in Europe. This third world, a question-mark world.

I was born of that first pre–World War II world in New York

City during the Depression. My mother's family had a good deal of money, and so did my father's. But as the depression deepened, things got tight financially. My father kept moving from job to job, trying always to find one that would make him a little more money to enable him to live in the manner that he had before. My mother, I think, was a good wife in many ways but was an increasingly discontented wife as the years went by. I can remember as a child hearing her say, "In my wildest dreams I never thought I'd have to live in a house with no servants." My father took that hard and kept trying to better himself one way or the other. We moved around from place to place all through my childhood. I think I went to a different school every year of my life until I went away to boarding school at the age of fourteen. There was no fixed point. Home was not for me a *place*. There was no house that was my house. Home was my parents, they were the one constant. When we moved, they always moved, of course, along with us. When there were fights—which there were, terrible fights as I remember, I can't remember the nature of what they were fighting about, but I remember the anger, the accusations from my mother about what she'd been reduced to by my father's not having the kind of job he should have, and my father's defenses—it was a matter of not just hearing two people fight, but I think as a child my terror was that if something blew them up, I would have no place to be. They were home. They were all there was that was, in any sense, constant in my life. I have good memories of my childhood certainly, but I think that the dark memories are memories of that terror.

I became a listener. I can remember as a child listening for the sounds in the house. Was that an angry sound or was that just a conversational sound? I was very aware of the atmosphere, always sort of frightened if something that had been planned would not come off because my parents would explode. So I think a lot of who I am to this day is because of those early days of anxiety and a sense of impending, if not doom, at least uncertainty. Where was I going to be next year? What would happen to this home that I lived in?

Then when I was ten years old, the great explosion I always feared took place early one morning on a Saturday. We were living at that point in a little town called Essex Fells, New Jersey, and my father had intended to take me and his mother, my grandmother Buechner, out to a football game that day, and though I've already written this out in other books, I'll tell it again anyway. I remember my brother and I woke up that Saturday morning because it was an exciting day, well at least one of us was going off to a football game and that was sort of exciting. We woke up as if it were Christmas morning, before dawn, too early to start opening the presents, or in the sense of this day, opening the sort of present the day was to be. We were playing with a roulette wheel someone had given us, I remember we put the green cloth with all the markings on the bed, and we were playing the roulette wheel. Then this funny memory—my brother and I've tried often to sort of bring it into focus without being able to bring it into real focus, it happened so long ago in 1936—of how the door to our bedroom opened. It was still just about dawn, I would say. Our father, we both agree, somehow appeared in the doorway. We have no recollection of anything he said or anything he did but just that he appeared. And then the door was shut, and we went on with our game. After a certain passage of time, there was this shout from below, and what had happened was my father committed suicide in the garage by turning on his car and killing himself with the exhaust. That was the bombshell.

Every family has something perhaps like that that blows everything sky high. It is the shadow cast by family, and even though this is fifty-six years later, it's still a shadow over me. I've worked at it and with it and written about it and thought about it and talked about it and had it exposed to loving, healing people, and yet still it's a part of who I am. I think almost a day doesn't go by without thinking about it. What happened then, and what perhaps is the reason why it remains a shadow, is that it was (as in so many dysfunctional families, to use that jargon phrase) a secret that we simply never told.

I mean, people knew, of course, that he had committed suicide, but as far as the world in which we moved was concerned, it was never talked about. We never talked about it to ourselves. And there was no religious dimension to our lives at all. Nobody went to church. My mother's mother, who I loved enormously, was a sort of freewheeling Unitarian, and she would go to church once in a while. Nobody was against it particularly, it just wasn't an issue. So when my father died, there was no funeral. There was no punctuation mark. He just disappeared. When different people would ask me how he died, or if the subject came up, I would say he died of heart trouble, which seemed a kind of truth. His heart was troubled, and he died.

So, my father's suicide was never talked about, nor did we talk about his life. We didn't talk about him at all. We didn't talk about what it had been like to be with him, to have him around. We didn't talk about what it was like not to have him around. It was almost as if he had not existed. I remember perhaps a year later coming up on my younger brother Jamie sitting by himself in his room and finding him in tears without any reason I could detect. I said, "Why are you crying?"

I couldn't imagine what had happened. He said, "I'm crying about Daddy," and that sort of rocked me on my feet because I had not cried about it. I didn't even have tears in me to cry about it at that point because it had become somehow a non-event, if I can put it like that.

The crying came much later, fifty years later.

■ ■ ■

My mother had a kind of wonderful, crazy wisdom, and she decided the thing to do was get the hell out, and not uncharacteristically of her she chose the island of Bermuda, a sunny tourist paradise that was far away but not too far away. So down we went. And my grandmother Buechner—who was one of her strongest and most vocal critics and always disapproved of my mother's extravagances; they had a marvelous sort of battle relationship—looked upon it as a terrible mistake, very characteristic of us to just up and go off to Never Never Land.

I suppose in some ways it was. But it was the saving of at least my life in a funny way because we moved out of this tragic situation, the darkness and the grief of it, to this magical island. And of all the places I've ever seen in my life, Bermuda is the one that when I think back on it I can almost *be* back on it. Its beauty was so great in those days before the Second World War, when the island was still without cars, if you can imagine, where there was nothing but horses, carriages, bicycles, sunshine, and all the rest of it. So it made it possible even more fully to forget the sadness, to forget the bomb that had exploded, the whole notion of beauty that is longing for something, beauty beyond beauty, for whatever beauty there is east of the sun and west of the moon.

There was still no religion in any sense in my life up to this point—no church, no feeling for it, nobody else going. But for some reason one of the little snapshots, one that I've mentioned already, that always sticks in my mind after these many, many years is me wheeling a bicycle up a Bermuda lane on a sort of dusky golden afternoon with the sun coming through the palms, and toward me came an Anglican priest looking like something out of Laurence Sterne with a broad-rimmed, flat black hat and black gaiters. He came up the lane and I went down, and why I should remember that all this time, I don't know. But it was just a glimpse, just a shadow of something perhaps someday to become important to me.

We would have probably stayed on in Bermuda for the rest of my childhood except that in September of 1939 a bomb went off in the world. Hitler invaded Czechoslovakia and Poland. The Second World War broke out, and all aliens in Bermuda, of which we were four, had to get out because the rumor went around immediately that the Germans were going to capture the island and make it into a submarine base from which to attack the American mainland. So off we went, back home to make a life for ourselves somewhere else.

We went back and settled finally in a little town in North Carolina called Tryon, which is in sort of the southwest corner of North Carolina not so far from Asheville, where my grandparents had some property. I remember loving it down there. As I say, the most important figure of my childhood in some ways, except for my mother, was her mother whom I called Naya. We've all had saints in our lives, by which I mean not plaster saints, not moral exemplars, not people setting for us a sort of suffocating good example, but I mean saints in the sense of life-givers, people through knowing whom we become more alive. She was one of my earliest saints, a marvelous articulate witty woman who spoke beautifully, spoke in paragraphs, had a great taste for literature, and a wonderful sense of humor, half-French-Swiss half New England. So we lived there with her, and that was one of the joys of it.

Then another of those moments happened that stick, like the priest in Bermuda, possibly pointing to something important in the future. Since we all, my brother and I and two little first cousins decided one day that since we'd never been baptized or christened, we ought to be. You know, you reach a certain stage and you move from short pants into long pants, you get a driver's license, and I thought it was time we should be baptized. So somehow we did it. I don't know who we went to see, but we got ahold of some Episcopal priest. I think our parents were perfectly willing to go along with this eccentricity because they came and we were christened, the four of us, in a little church on Melrose Avenue in Tryon, North Carolina. I'd love to know, if I could look back and really see, why was it I thought that was something to do? I don't know, but it seemed important at the time, so I did it.

Speaking about Naya, my grandmother, I think often that the relationship between grandchildren and their grandparents is apt to be so much easier, richer, than the relationship between child and parent because somehow just that remove in generation lets a lot of air in. There's not the same possibility for making terrible mistakes. I can't put it quite right, but it was certainly true of us. I think my mother loved me in large part because she needed me so much. I became her husband, her father, her confessor, her adversary, all the things my father might have been had he been there was sort of foisted upon me. And I loved her and I needed her, but she loved me, I think, not so much for who I was as for the empty place that I filled in her life. My grandmother, on the other hand, didn't have so many empty places in her life. She was wonderfully serene. I can see her. She smoked Chesterfield cigarettes in white cigarette holders, and I can see her sitting out on a terrace with the Blue Ridge Mountains before her. The world was going to pieces around her in the sense of the European war, but she never turned a hair. So she was one of my saints. But my mother, despite in many ways being a very bad mother, needing me as she did, one of her great gifts to me was when she sent me off to boarding school because she thought I should have men in my life, I should have fathers in my life, and I should get away from home. That must have been quite difficult for her, I would think, but she did it.

I went off to a school called Lawrenceville, a boarding school in New Jersey. It was just the best place for me to have gone because it was full of fathers really, good men, crazy some of them, but interesting and interested and full of strength, which was strengthening to me. It was there that I began for the first time to sort of talk about the family secret. It was my little treasure, my little dark treasure. I would trot it out and show it to new friends, and that somehow sealed friendships.

It was at Lawrenceville that I experienced another sort of cryptic moment. I guess I knew enough about the Episcopal church to know that the next step after being christened was to be confirmed. I looked at my calendar, I guess, and figured the time had come for that. I don't remember any sort of religious impulse in the sense of any real reaching out of my spirit, but somehow something said to me, "It's time." So I attended a confirmation class, which was available at the school. The time came, and the bishop of New Jersey, a wonderful man named Gardner—I can see him still, a great bull-like man, florid, sort of medieval, somewhere between a bishop and an executioner—confirmed me at the chapel in Lawrenceville.

When the time came, I went off to college, to Princeton where my father had gone and it was possible to get a scholarship because we really had no money to speak of. We were living pretty much on the charity of my father's mother, who disapproved so strongly of my mother's extravagances that it was always a constant fear maybe someday she'd turn off the tap, and then we'd be penniless. But I was able to get a scholarship to Princeton and off I went. I was there two years before and two years after my time in the Army, very different times.

The first two years were just one marvelous drunken party after the other. Everybody was getting drafted or enlisting, so nobody took studies very seriously because who was to say whether you'd live long enough to reap the rewards. It was a wonderful time. I didn't learn anything that I can remember. If a night went by that you didn't throw up, you figured it had been a night wasted. Then off to the Army I went for two years of very undistinguished service, all of it at several different places in the United States, and I ended up of all things the chief of the statistical section in Camp Pickett, Virginia. I knew about as much about statistics as I know about the other side of the moon. Afterward, I came back to Princeton, as did most of my friends, with a sort of different attitude. We'd had enough of throwing up, and it was so nice to be out of the Army and back into regular clothes again that I did certainly study and was interested in my courses.

There was one key scene that I have always remembered out of many other such scenes that I've forgotten: I was down at the Nassau Tavern drinking beer with a group of people when one boy I didn't know very well made a remark using the name of Christ with such obscenity and blasphemy that it practically threw me off my chair. I thought, "I've got to go somewhere to cleanse myself of what I just heard." I didn't say anything to him, but I was just appalled. I remember getting on my bike at about one o'clock in the morning thinking I had to go to a church, to just go into it. So I went to one after another and, wonderful irony, they were all locked. But there was one church on lower Nassau Street that, though locked, had a stone balustrade up the side, and by crawling up that I could look at least in the window, and I could see the altar where a light was kept lit. That was a comforting sight, an important moment just glimpsing through the window. Talk about life as a parable—needing desperately to find a church, and they're all locked, but there was this one window, which I looked through.

Finally I graduated and took a job teaching English at my old boarding school, Lawrenceville, which was wonderful. At some point in that period, for reasons again that I don't remember exactly, I felt unclean, uncertain, at sea, and somebody told me about this monastery in New York State on the Hudson River called the Order of the Holy Cross. I was told a wonderful priest was there who was wise and holy and who would be useful to talk to. So I went up only to discover that this priest that I'd gone to see had taken a special vow of silence and could not be talked to or even seen. Sort of like the church was locked. And the guest master, the old monk who was there to deal with guests like me, was available but he'd had a stroke. He couldn't speak in a way that I could understand. Talk about parables! So what I found in that monastery was not what I had gone to find, which were answers to my questions, I suppose. What I found instead was silence, which in a way was much better because if I'd found the answers to my questions, whatever my questions were, I would have only come away with a few answers that I would've forgotten just as completely as I've forgotten the names of the people who might've given them to me.

■ ■ ■

Words. Who gives a hoot about words? Like Job asking God, "Why do things happen to a man like me, these terrible things, my children dead, my cattle gone?" Supposing God had said, "Look, Job, I'll tell you, here's why it happened . . ." So what? Would that have helped Job? Of course not. What Job needed was what he got, which was the vision of God himself. "I had heard of you by the hearing of my ears; now mine eyes have beheld thee." That was the answer that was without words. So in a funny way I didn't get the answer, but I got silence, the sense of mystery, the sense of holiness. Nobody talked to me at all, except at the end I went to see the father who had the stroke, and he was able to say to me, "Do you go to church regularly now? Do you confess your sins?" I said, "No." "Would you like to confess them?" I said I guessed I would, and I said a few little things I could think of. And then he said, "Well, you know you have a long way to go," and he was right, and I still do. But I remember that, "You have a long way to go."

CHAPTER 6

HOLY MOMENTS

After that I left Lawrenceville and returned to New York to our little apartment on 74th Street, which has become the ancestral home, to become a full-time writer. The home has been in our family now a long time. My mother had it first in 1946, forty-six years ago, and we've always had it. But anyway, there I went, and I couldn't write anything. With all the time in the world to do what I wanted most to do, I found it impossible to do it. I fell in love with a girl, and that took a lot of time. I sort of floundered around the city, unable to write much of anything, and by a fluke, my apartment was just a block away from a church called the Madison Avenue Presbyterian Church. I think I must have heard that the preacher of that church was supposed to be very good at his job. He was a man named George Arthur Buttrick. So with nothing else to do and with no motive as far as I can remember more serious than just to try to pass the time—I was by myself, my book wasn't going well, I was in love with a girl who didn't love me—I had to do something on Sunday, and church didn't cost anything much.

So I started going to hear Buttrick, and he was a spell-binder, most impressive. Just the reverse of big-time, hard-sell preaching, he sort of had a funny, cracked, oatmealy kind of voice with a faint Scottish accent way in the background. He twitched, and his glasses glittered. He moved around in awkward ways in the pulpit. You never knew where he was going. He didn't have a three-point sermon. You had no idea that there were three points or six points or two points. But he prepared them very, very carefully. I remember him saying how long it took him to write a sermon, but there was no sense of that. It was as if they just flowed out of him. He was articulate. He was well-read. He was fascinating, and I was fascinated. Sunday after Sunday I would go to hear that man, overwhelmed by him in many ways.

And then there came this one particular Sunday, which I've often written about like everything else, but I'll tell you about it again. It was the year, 1953, that Elizabeth became the queen, and that was sort of the theme, I think, underlying what Buttrick was talking about. He mentioned the coronation of Elizabeth in Westminster Abbey, and then he said, "Of course, Jesus was offered a crown by Satan on that hill when Satan said, 'If only you will do this and that, all the kingdom of the earth will be yours.'" He said that unlike Elizabeth, Jesus turned down that crown. "But," said Buttrick—and up to this point it was just a regular sermon, seemed to me—"though he refused the crown that was offered to him by Satan, he nonetheless is crowned again and again in the hearts of people who believe in him." And even up to that point it seemed to me nothing one would not expect from a sermon, but Buttrick continued, "Jesus is crowned again and again in the hearts of those who believe in him amidst confession and tears and great laughter." When the phrase "great laughter" came out, Jesus crowned amidst confession, tears, and great laughter, some wall inside me crumbled. I remember I was just bowled over.

I remember tears springing from my eyes. Laughter at the coronation of Christ.

I think from that day to this I've never known altogether what that laughter is all about. It's laughter of incredulity, I think. It should be true, maybe it's true, maybe he was who we think he was. The laughter of Abraham and Sarah when they were going to have a child—they laughed so hard in Genesis. Maybe it's true, maybe it's all too good to be anything but true that brings with it the laughter of relief and release. Yes, it's true, and what a difference that makes.

I was so overwhelmed by what Buttrick said that I remember going up to have lunch with my grandmother Buechner and telling her about it. She came from a German background of free thinkers and atheists who'd come over here after those little revolutions in 1848 and settled in Brooklyn. I said, "This wonderful thing has happened. I've got to do something. I've got to join." I could see she was sort of puzzled, and she said, "Well, I'm so pleased for you. You know, maybe there's something to it."

But there was so much to it for me that I had to do something. It was not enough just to receive it, I had to respond to it somehow. So I don't know how long afterward, but I found my way to the office of Dr. Buttrick and I told him something of what I had felt. I said, "I think I'm going to have to go to a seminary because I don't know anything about Christ. I've never really read the Bible." I don't remember much of what Buttrick said, but I do remember him saying something like, "It would be a shame to lose a good novelist for the sake of making a mediocre preacher. You don't really have to go to a seminary, you know. If you want to find out more, join the church. We have a class for new members, read the Bible, things like that." But I said somehow that didn't seem enough. I had to do something more dramatic than that because the thing that had happened to me was so dramatic. So I persisted, and he said, "All right, if you feel that way, get your hat." He got his, and he drove me in his own little car. This was a great big busy New York church with several other ministers and secretaries and all the hoopla that goes on in churches. He drove me himself in his little car all the way up Madison Avenue and Fifth Avenue around the top of the park to 120th Street and Broadway to Union Seminary and introduced me to whoever it was, John Knox, I think, who was some sort of a dean. As a result of that, I decided to go there, and it was a great gift.

Talk about saints in your life. I never knew Buttrick really as a human being. We met a few times, but he was a life-giver for me. That's all I can say, both as a preacher and as this wonderfully generous man. Imagine some young idiot coming in and saying, "I think I'd like to go to seminary," and him saying, "All right I'll take you up there," after having first tried to persuade me I didn't really have to do that. But it was one of the major moves in my life, really, to go to a seminary. My education at Princeton insofar as I had any education at all, was absolutely sort of slapdash. It was like a great smorgasbord of courses. I took a little bit of this and a little bit of that because they had wonderful titles like, "Love and Death in the American Novel" and "Cultural Anthropology." I just liked the sounds of these things, but I didn't learn anything much. When I went to Union, I was so motivated because I was at that point so on fire with, I can only say, Christ. I was to the point where when I would see his name on a page, it was like seeing the face of somebody you loved, and my heart would beat faster. I had to find out more about him.

■ ■ ■

So up I went, and I couldn't have chosen a better place because that was the golden age of Union Seminary. Paul Tillich was there, and Reinhold Niebuhr, and people whose names aren't as well-known were also there, like James Muilenburg, who was also one of my saints—an Old Testament professor of enormous power . . . he *was* the Old Testament. He would act out the great dramas, and when he stood in that huge lecture hall at Union Seminary, people flooding in from practically the street to hear him, and would describe the creation of God saying, "*Yehi!*" or "Let there be light," light came in . . . that's all you can say. Every face lit up because somehow he made it happen.

It was almost unimaginably exciting for me to be at Union, and I loved it. I went there for three years assuming that what I would do, because that's what people in the seminaries did do, was become a minister and have a church. I was prepared to do that while recognizing there were an awful lot of things about having a church that I'm not very good at. I'd never even been a member of a church except briefly Buttrick's church. I don't know how to run one; I don't know what goes on in one. I don't know about budgets, I don't know about committees, and I wouldn't be any good. But still, that was what you did after you went to seminary. That's what I would have done, I think, except that again a sort of flukish thing happened. I had a letter from somebody saying that Phillips Exeter Academy, this school in New Hampshire for boys then, now coed, was looking for somebody to come and start a religion department. This man knew that I was just about to be ordained, but he knew also that I had taught at Lawrenceville and had a turn of mind. So he said, "Wouldn't this be the perfect job for you?" I decided maybe he was right.

The next move was to Exeter, and just before this, I should say, I got married to my wife, Judy. We lived in New York during those years when I was going back to Union Seminary and then we moved up to Exeter in 1958.

■ ■ ■

The '50s and '60s were a turbulent time in the history of our country, especially in the history of the young people of our country: the great protests against Vietnam, the great civil rights demonstrations, the great sit-ins on college campuses and so on. Exeter was a highly competitive school, terribly hard to get into, so the kids who were there were brighter than you can even imagine, infinitely brighter than I was because when you're that young, you have so few things to clutter your mind with. You just know what you know. They hated the country, they hated the Vietnam War, they hated their parents, they hated the school particularly, and they especially hated religion because all the other people there were saying how good it was for them. Also there was a rule at Exeter in those days that every boy had to attend church, either the school church or some church of his own choice, and that's hardly the way to create a receptive congregation. They were there against their wills, not liking the infringement of their freedom, and they were right—it was an infringement. But it worked in my benefit because I was there primarily to start a religion department with courses just as demanding and rigorous and academic and respectable as courses in math, English, science, and so on.

The sort of antireligious sentiment actually worked in my benefit because the kids were out to destroy me, not personally so much as a representative of the church, and the only representative in that very secular school. And the only way to get at me to destroy me was to take my courses, which were electives. If it hadn't been for their destructive intent—if the only kids who'd taken my courses were the sort of churchy, good little straight arrows, the *possos* (Exeter slang for those who were positive about more or less everything. *Negos*, of which there were thousands, were the ones who were negative about everything), it would've been the kiss of death. It would've confirmed everybody's, including the faculty's, darkest suspicions that this was a sort of catechetical class where questions were taught together with the answers.

But instead all the dark eminences of the campus came and took these courses. They were the ones who also had to come to church because that was the rule. It was terrifying, but what made it such a marvelous way to begin a ministry was that they were so sharp you couldn't get away with any of the nonsense that preachers get away with all the time. You couldn't be sentimental, you couldn't be fuzzy, you couldn't be illogical, and you couldn't be irrelevant because those *scorpions* were there to pounce upon you. They weren't all that way, but there were a lot of them that way. You had to pretty much speak what sounded at least perhaps as the truth, if only the truth of your own feelings about religious matters. It was a wonderful thing.

That was true both in the classroom and also particularly in church. Once in a while when a sermon was being preached, maybe by me or by other preachers from different traditions I would bring in, you'd look out at those faces and you could see that those kids, in spite of themselves, were listening, couldn't help but listen. Even if they weren't buying any of it, they were at least listening to it. My one argument in favor of required church—which in every other sense I could only agree with the boys, that it was an outrage to make somebody go to church—was that I would rather have a shot at those unwilling little targets than to think that nobody would ever have a shot at them. Maybe something would come through, even if they were there against their will and hating it. Maybe something would come through. And who knows what does come through or what doesn't come through.

One of these was a boy named John Irving who went on to write *A Prayer for Owen Meany*, among other books. In the front of *Owen Meany*, there's a little acknowledgment of people he felt he wanted to thank for something or other, and I was among them. He stands for this mystery of who's to say what gets through. He was a student in a couple of my courses. I remember him but didn't know him well, he was a little shy, sort of a pimply little kid, a faculty child, which was a hard row to hoe. He didn't speak much. I remember, I think I was the only person he knew who'd ever written a book, so he brought me some little stories he'd written of which I remember nothing. But anyway in the thirty or forty years since, he felt called upon to thank me for this.

So something got through, I suppose. And it gives one pause to think in your life of the people whom you've had an enormous influence on for good or for ill—that's the scary part. Something you said or didn't say or you did or failed to do, which made all the difference.

During this time, another of those divine moments happened to me—a divine moment . . . you never want to be too sure it's God who's talking to you or what it is he said, you never want to try to formalize it, because it's always a mystery, isn't it?—but anyway, I found myself going to a conference led by a woman named Agnes Sanford, who had been billed to me by an Episcopal priest as a remarkable woman. He said, "If there is such a thing as a real faith healer, she's the real thing. You ought to go listen to her." So I went. And she was the real thing, there was no question about it. You just had to look at her to see that whatever she was saying, she was saying because she had known it to be true, at least in her own experience.

She talked about prayer in a way that I'd never heard it talked about before. She said, "Ministers especially are so bad at praying because they never ask for anything, really, except for the general things—bless this group and bless that and thank you for this. They're always afraid to ask for anything for fear they won't get it and that that will somehow shake their own faith and shake the faith of the congregation; so they pray sort of bland, formal prayers." She said the vision she had was of Jesus standing with his hands tied behind his back, unable to do anything because nobody dared ask him to do anything. She said, "Go ahead and ask for anything. Ask for healing, ask to be healed. Don't worry about the little voice inside of you that says, *It's not going to happen* or *God doesn't listen to things like that* or *How do you think you're going to change God?* Don't worry about that little voice. Of course, that little voice is there. It's a product of centuries of skepticism, doubt, and all that. Just drown it out with your prayers and pray for miracles."

She had enormous success not only as a physical healer, but also, increasingly as she grew old, as what she called a healer of memories. She was wonderfully un-Madame Blavatskian—there was nothing spooky about her. She didn't wear a beaded shawl or have a crystal ball. She was just a little woman, with a puffy little face. I could see her sort of running a bridge club. She said anybody who wanted to come to her could be healed; she

91

would receive. So I went to her for a healing of my memories, and I told her about my father and so on. What she'd do is pray in the most conversational, unfancy, unprayerful kind of way, and she'd speak this image into her prayers. The image was of the person she was praying for, a house with rooms and corridors; some of the rooms hadn't been opened for years and were full of dark places. She would invite Jesus into the house, saying, "Now open the doors and let in the fresh air, blessing it, cleansing it, and making it livable again." She prayed this prayer for me, and it was a very powerful moment for me, not only in terms of specifically what she'd asked for, my healing, but the notion that prayer was real. It wasn't just giving God something you didn't need or want, but it was opening yourself to the mystery of this extraordinary power to work through you into the lives of others, a big moment. I found myself for the first time really daring to pray for people who came to me for help, as she always did and as Jesus did before her, with her hands on the head of the person and praying for healing.

■ ■ ■

I left Exeter for the good Protestant reason that I was enjoying it too much. We'd been there for nine years, and everything was going well. I did what I did well enough so that everybody was pleased and complimentary, and we had lots of good friends. But at least part of the reason for leaving (this is where you suspect your own storytelling so much; I'm sure there were many other reasons) among others was this one, that was since everything was going so well, there would be no reason ever to do anything differently or better or more wisely as long as I stayed there because it was like being in a lovely warm tub, and therefore I'd better move on and make myself do something different and better.

Also, of course, I had this tremendous hankering to get back to writing because I had to put that aside. I wrote one novel while I was at Exeter called *The Final Beast*, but that was only one novel. That was, I guess, my fourth book. So, I thought, "I'll try my hand as a writer again."

So we left Exeter with many, many regrets and went up to Vermont where I've really, in effect, lived ever since. I know the first year we lived in Vermont I was desperately trying to write a book. It's always so desperate to write a book, but especially desperate because I had to do something to justify my having left this job I loved and everybody thinking, "What's old Buechner going to do up there now, going to do anything at all?" It was the year that Martin Luther King Jr. was assassinated and then shortly afterward Bobby Kennedy was assassinated, and I thought if there's anything this world really doesn't need, it's another stupid book. I'm a minister; I should be doing something that makes sense. I almost came apart, all sorts of strange doubts, dreads, and hypochondria. I suddenly was isolated. I had nobody much except my wife and children to bounce my life off of, but I managed to finish a sort of strangled book, which was published.

Then one of those things, again one of those moments, came in the form of a letter from a man named Charles Price who was then what they called the Preacher of the University at Harvard, the chaplain in effect, asking me if I would give a series of lectures they'd had there for a long, long time called the Noble Lectures, which had always before been given by theologians, except for the first one who was Teddy Roosevelt. How he got to be invited, I can't imagine; maybe he had a

theological side. But anyway, a number of theological lumi-
naries had given them, and I had no illusions about myself
as a theologian—I taught prep school, and that was about it.
So I wrote Charlie Price back again and said, "Well, that's a
very flattering invitation, but I'm not really a theologian. What
would you think I might talk about?" In his letter back he said,
"I would think something in the area of religion and letters."

Religion and letters. And of course by letters, he meant literature, but by some happy chance I thought of letters as *a b c
d e f* g and on up to *z*. Religion in the alphabet. And it was out
of sort of trying to put back into some sort of shape the notion
that God speaks to us in what happens to us that I realized the
events of our lives are a kind of alphabet. It's a hard alphabet
to decipher, because like the Hebrew alphabet, there are no
vowels—you sort of have to fill it in, have to imagine what the
vowels are, have to figure out where one word ends and another
word starts. And there are gutturals in Hebrew, and there are
sibilants, and harsh tones. Anyway, after having nearly driven
myself to a nervous breakdown trying to write this novel, what
I suddenly decided to do was to try to write about this, my
life as an alphabet, all of our lives as an alphabet, as a series of
events through which God is trying to say something.

I called the lectures, and then the book which they became,
The Alphabet of Grace. God as grace speaks to us through what
happens. I went to Harvard and delivered them. What I did
was take a representative day of my life—getting up, waking
up the children, going to the john, having breakfast, going off
to work, kissing my wife good-bye, coming back, and this, that,
and the other, going to bed, going to sleep—just a representative day and listening to whatever it was that was holy in it. I
admire my courage in retrospect because there I was standing

in this exalted place, preceded by all these distinguished theologians, and talking about waking my children up, going to the john, having breakfast, and so on, but I did it. And it was a key moment for me because it turned me, literally speaking and for the first time, to my own life as a source of treasure. It's out of that experience that the autobiographical books came, where I looked back on a certain section of my life and asked the same question, "What was there in it of God?"

So I wrote these autobiographical books in which, like Leo Bebb, I exposed my secrets, telling everything about the past in greater detail. Everything except about my mother, because she was surviving. She survived until she was about ninety-three years old and in many ways did it very well. She survived by simply shutting the past off the way you might lock the door; she simply would not talk about it except once in a while she might say a few things. But anyway, I could not tell her story so I could not tell my story in its fullness for fear of it somehow destroying her, or even more, for fear that she would destroy me, such was her power.

I remember when my novel *The Return of Ansel Gibbs* came out, a book in which I mentioned in a very fictional and oblique way my father's suicide. A very minor part of it has to do with the suicide of a character who doesn't even appear in the book. She was so angry that when I came down with my new young bride to visit my mother, she almost wouldn't speak to me. I remember she said, "Someday I'm going to get you off in the woods and tell you what I think about that terrible thing you did." I was so under her power that it never occurred to me to say that my father's death was as much my story to tell as it was her story not to tell. I didn't even think about that.

These things that are negative give you such a bad impression of her because they were true, but I have to say that she was also a woman of great charm, beauty, a wonderful sense of humor, tremendously good company, the companion of my youth—all of these things. But she was a woman crippled by her beauty in a way. If you're beautiful, people come to you just because you're beautiful. You don't have to be nice or kind or interested or sympathetic. They come just to bask in the light of your beauty, and she was sort of hurt by that.

One of the other moments where something broke through for me—like going to the monastery, like for some reason choosing to be christened at the age of whatever I was—was this incident that took place when I was teaching at Lawrenceville before I had any notion of going to a seminary. I was to have dinner with my mother, and I'd come into New York for that purpose. I hadn't seen her for a while, I think, and she'd sort of gotten things all pulled together. The apartment looked nice, and she had cooked a nice little meal and had the silver candlesticks on the table. We were just about to sit down for supper when the phone rang. It was for me, which was surprising as it was her apartment. And it was a friend of mine with whom I had taught at Lawrenceville, and almost immediately I heard to my horror that he was in tears. It scared me out of my wits, because how do you ever deal with somebody's tears, especially somebody I had no reason to think had cause for tears? He was calling because there'd been a terrible automobile accident on the West Coast in which his mother, his father, and his pregnant sister had all been involved, and he wasn't sure that any of them would live. He was flying out to see what he could do, if there was anything to do. He was at the airport, and he asked could I come and just sit with him until the plane took off.

Instead of saying yes just like that, which any normal person would've done, thinking of my mother in the other room and this meal that she'd prepared, I said, "Just . . . will you call back in five minutes? I've just got to go talk to my mother." So I went back and I told her this story, and her reaction was absolutely ridiculous. "He's a grown man. He's behaving like a child. I've got this wonderful dinner prepared, and we haven't seen each other in a long time. He'll be perfectly all right." And what was so horrifying about it was not just that she said it, but that I'd already said it to myself. It was a real watershed. I'd said all those things to myself. How absurd. Then this revelation—and again I distrust my own narration . . . did it happen right then, did it happen later, had it been happening for a long time and only sort of triggered then?—that not to go into the world's pain, not to go see my friend, not to somehow offer him whatever cup of cold water I could, to play it safe, to stay with my mother, to have a nice dinner was not only for the world's sake a disaster, but for my sake a disaster. To play it safe, to stay home where the candles are lit and the meal is prepared was to have your life somehow diminished. To go out into the world, even if the world scares the hell out of you, and bores you to death, and intimidates you, and confuses you—that is the *only* life. Somehow I saw that, I felt that, knew it through that moment. Again, ironies like the locked church and the silent monastery. When the phone rang again, he said, "Don't come down. My plane is leaving in twenty minutes; I'm off. It's just good to talk to you." And so the moment passed and no harm was done, I think. But great good was also done.

CHAPTER 7

BETTER
THAN I USED TO BE,
BUT FAR FROM
WELL

My three daughters, my wife, and I were living in this beautiful part of Vermont, rich, blessed, everybody healthy, very close, loving, did things together; and I always thought, *This won't last*, because that was what I learned in my childhood, that good things don't last, that there is always something waiting. There was a green hill as you looked out east from our house over the Green Mountains on the property of a neighbor of ours, which had sort of a spine down one end. This neighbor said it always looked to him like a huge shaggy green beast browsing its way through the valley in our direction, though you couldn't see its head because it was down beneath the hill in front of it. I always thought that was a very vivid image, and I thought, *Someday the beast will find us, probably. It's found lots of other people.*

In one sense, the beast did find us. Our oldest daughter, in her late teens I guess, became anorexic, a gradual process of not eating very much. We'd say, "Oh, for heaven's sake, you ought to have another piece of that," or "You can't go without breakfast," and so on. She went away to college, to Princeton, for a while and it got worse. Anyway, I won't go through all the details but she was married in the process of this to a boy we loved. And as it turned out, the anorexia destroyed the marriage. I can only sympathize with the boy—it would've destroyed my marriage too. When my daughter was off on the West Coast, she became so skeletal. We'd sort of seen her a little bit off and on, but one day the phone rang and a doctor from a hospital in Seattle said that they needed parental permission to feed her against her will through her nose because otherwise she would die.

You love all your children equally, I suppose, but she was my first child. She had made me a father, and I loved her as much as I've ever loved anybody. So this was a devastating word to hear. My love for her was like sort of my mother's love for me, too possessive, too much for my sake. Part of what I think my daughter was doing was to say, "Let me go. Let me be free. The one place I'm free is with my own body. You at least can't tell me what to eat. I'll damn well eat what I want." Part of her trouble was me. My love was a controlling love, a needful love. The people who loved her right because they weren't emotionally involved were the hospital people, the psychiatrist, the one who fed her through her nose, and the people in AA because anorexia led to alcoholism as well. They loved her right, tough love, love confronting her with the fact that she was dying. By a gradual process, she became well, and at this moment, God willing, remains well and alive and one of the most creative, fun, solid, wise people I know. She's my role model, I told her the other day.

She survived, and better than survived. But I was still sick—sick with anxiety, sick with the need I had somehow for my children to be around me, to make my life full. I knew myself she was well and I was still sick, a bizarre thing. One day she told me she had had so much help from AA that I really ought to try one of these twelve-step programs. I thought that seemed sort of dim, but I did finally try it. And it was a tremendous help to me to be with people who do speak the truth with love, who tell their stories in ways that somehow resonate with your stories. You look at these faces of people who have much more horrifying stories to tell than I do, who somehow come through them. They've come through it because of each other and because, as they say, of their higher power. They've found a power, if only in the group, greater than their own power to heal them. So that was one thing that helped me get better.

And then of course therapy. I also did that, and it was also very helpful in many, many ways. Just finding myself in a place so safe with this one person that I was able to talk about things I'd never talked about at all before with anybody. I'm not well, but I'm better than I was. One day I had the feeling that, by her questions, my therapist was trying to lead me to an insight that was going to be of great importance. But I wasn't answering them right, or I wasn't understanding them right, and I finally said to her, "Maggie, you're trying to get me to see something. Can you just tell me what it is? I'm not getting it." And she said, "Well, that's really not the way therapy works. You've got to wait till it sort of emerges." But by the end of the hour she said, "Well, all right. I'll tell you what it is," and I can hardly imagine any point of my life at which I was more interested in hearing an insight because, as far as I knew, my survival depended on it. And she told me what it was. I have no idea what she said, and the issue had nothing to do with her skill as a therapist. It's a cliché, and it's so true—I literally wasn't ready to hear. I heard the words but I have no idea what she said.

Some years later I found myself with another therapist, as it turns out, also a woman who was very, very useful in a great many ways. Her branch of therapy involves something called psychosynthesis, which is the notion that we're all composed of many selves. We can all of us recognize that, I think—there's the professional self, the face you show to public; there's the self you show your family; there's the child's self that survives, and so on, and to recognize these selves, to try to make peace among them, to realize each one is going to contribute is the thing. But the trick is not to let, for instance, the child drive the machine of you for fairly obvious reasons. That was very useful, this sort of inner-child business. It's too bad all these things have become such jargon buzzwords, but at the time it was new to me.

There was a child, the little boy who was bowled over by this explosion of his father's suicide and never talked about it, and for the first time really during those two therapy sessions, I not only told about it, but I finally—finally!—cried about it. Oh, what a relief. This second therapist brought me through the business of getting closure with my parents. Even though by then my mother had died, speaking the truth of them even in their absence and hearing the truth of them was good.

■ ■ ■

I had a dream about my mother that sort of grew out of that therapy. She died just a little bit ago in her apartment in New York City, and as I said, she survived, and she survived well, despite the fact that she closed herself off from the world. I think she was so full of guilt about her marriages—my father's suicide, two other marriages, one of which ended in divorce and the other one would've ended in divorce if her husband hadn't died—that she sort of closed herself off from the world. She moved to New York City, kept her name out of the phone book, and became extremely deaf, which is such a tragic thing because it became impossible to talk to her about anything that mattered. You can't shout subtleties. You can't shout feelings. You can only talk about shoutable things. Even then, when she talked to you, she closed her eyes. So she couldn't hear you very well and she didn't see you. She didn't see any real friends because she got to be so old most of them were dead, and because she kept her name out of the phonebook, the ones who were left couldn't find her. And all of that suggests what it was: a very limited life. It also suggests somebody walled up in a prison and bitterness and narrowness, but she was none of those things. She was tremendous fun. She kept in touch with us, her immediate family, and we loved to see her. She had a terrible tongue when she was angered; she could destroy you. When she struck, she struck to kill. She would say appalling things, kind of frightening things, which is why I never dared write about her until after she was dead. But after she was dead, I not only wrote about her, but I had this dream about her, which was sort of my closure with her, except that it wasn't. You're never through with the dead, and they're never through with you, in my experience.

> The dream was set in the bedroom of her apartment on 79th Street, only the room had been cleared at last of all the years of her accumulating. The furniture, the pictures, the things under beds and in closets, the clothes, the boxes, the old

letters—they were all gone. It was superbly empty now. The walls and ceiling had been repainted white. The floors had been waxed and polished. The dusty venetian blinds were gone, and the sunlight came sliding in through the windows and made clear, geometric shapes on the bare walls. All the dramas that had taken place in that room were over and done with. All the life my mother had lived there and the death she had died there were over and done with too. I thought how now there could be new tenants there, new life. Then suddenly my mother was there, and my brother, Jamie, and I were there with her. My brother reached out and patted her as she went by as if to show me she was real. She was paying no particular attention to either of us. She looked very well, in her thirties or early forties maybe. She was getting ready to go out some place, and all of her energies were being devoted to that end. She was fussing about her hair, her clothes. She said she had to meet a woman somewhere and didn't want to be late. She even named the woman, who was somebody I knew she'd particularly disliked for over sixty years, which helps me believe that maybe the Kingdom of Heaven was where she was and is. That's all I can remember her saying, and that's about all there was to the dream.

It didn't seem a very important dream to me at the time, but what it said to me was important. I think it said that my mother was somehow back in business. It said that there was no need to worry about her anymore. When she was alive, the rule she laid down—all the more devastating of course by never saying it in so many words—was that my brother and I had no right to be happy as long as she was unhappy. The dream said that was over with now. She had her business to get back to. My brother and I had ours.[2]

The most important part of the dream, in a funny way, was the recognition of the rule: You have no right to be happy unless I am happy. You have no right to talk about the past because that makes me unhappy even if it makes you happy. Of course we internalize those rules. And I think the rule had not only been internalized by me to the point where my happiest times were always marred, shadowed, but I expanded it to a rule that said it was all right to be happy as long as everybody for whom you feel responsible is happy too. And that's a terrible curse to sail under.

You have every right to be happy. Dostoevsky said through Father Zosima in *The Brothers Karamazov*, "Anybody who is completely happy can be sure he's doing God's will on earth." We are called to be happy, not only for our own sakes but because that's what life is all about. That's why the morning stars threw down their spears and sang for joy. You're not only called to be happy for your sake, but you're called to be happy for everybody's sake. How much more help I could have been to my anorexic daughter if I had been happy, at peace, whole, a rock, instead of a haggard, anxiety-ridden, doom-ridden cripple.

■ ■ ■

I'm better than I used to be, but far from well. The journey continues; I do what I can. The great problem is to try to live in the present, not the past, not the future, but in the now. The trees are waving outside in the breeze, an emblem of what I try to do now, try to notice that there are trees. They're waving right now. Try to bless your demons and let them go away. Demons, anxiety, desire, things you never did, let them go and think about things you did do. Try to let go and let God, that wonderful old slogan. And to listen for God, that still, small voice, so still that maybe sometimes you wonder if there's any God there at all. I wish God would talk sometimes so I could hear him. I wish, as Woody Allen wonderfully jokes, that sometimes he'd just clear his throat. But just enough whispers in the wings, the strange coincidence, the miraculous happenstance, the right saint coming by at the right time, to me means that the stillness of God is the stillness he has to preserve, because if he were to speak, it'd blow everything sky high.

Shakespeare can't enter *Hamlet*, Rembrandt can't enter a canvas, except in the terms of the canvas or the play. But Shakespeare can enter the play by writing it, by putting himself into characters, and in this way Rembrandt also can enter his canvases by way of using his brush and imagination. So too the way God can deal with the world is elusively, whispers in the wings, subtly, suggestively, never coercing, just waving like the trees in time. So I try to listen for that.

John Updike wrote, "God saves his deepest silence for his saints." I'm not a saint, and I've never heard his deepest silence, thank God. At the same time I've recognized sometimes how my faith, my belief, is very much of the mind and of the heart also. Emotion is certainly involved, but I've never had stomach faith. I've never had the vision. I've never been struck. Well, even though I say that, I almost have to unsay it because there have been moments when I almost was struck. Like the moment when Buttrick talked about confession, tears, and great laughter—I think I knew God was there with me as concretely as I knew that I was sitting in that church in New

York City, I knew that there was a power of such preciousness, beauty, truth, and love that I couldn't contain myself.

So I'm almost unsaying what I started to say. I was going to say that my faith, like my doubt, mostly involves my mind and not my stomach. Basically that's true. I can't really imagine what it would be like to behold the Lord and not as a stranger. I'm not a saint, so I haven't had that experience. And yet, even as a not-saint, I get glimpses. I think we all have, and may there be many more of them for all of us.

CHAPTER 8

THE PRESENCE OF PEACE

I do not know much about prayer, that's for sure, but I pray a lot because I move around the world, so I can't help but do that. The kind of prayer I do at night, if I'm not so sleepy that I forget to do it, is thinking about how in the evening, if you're like me, almost everybody in the world turns on the news to listen to what's going on in the world that day. And it seems to me as I listen to it, the same kinds of things are always going on—there's always a war going on somewhere and by the same token there's always a search for peace. And there's always a problem of hunger and homelessness.

It seems to me that one could do worse as a form for prayer at night, when you turn out the light and wait for sleep to wash over you like a tide, to think back over the news of your day, that particular day that's coming to an end. To remember not just the wars fought on a national scale, but also the wars that we're all of us engaged in—aggressive wars to gain control, to get the upper hand, to have the last word, to get our way, fought not with weapons or even letters, but with silences and tones of voice and all the ways we know of fighting with each other.

We're often at war with the people we love the best. We often engage in wars with no particular goal in sight, but rather for the sort of dark pleasure of fighting a war between husbands and wives, between parents and children, between friends. In these aggressive wars and defensive wars we all, I think to some degree, fight to survive. We camouflage ourselves very often in ways that don't suggest we are indeed really warring at all. But at the end of the day, as you look back over your wars, ask yourself, How did your wars go today? Who were you fighting today? How did they work out? Did you deliver the knockout blow? Was it worth it? Were you knocked out? What does winning a war with somebody mean? What does losing a war with somebody mean?

■ ■ ■

I fought a war one whole summer with my youngest daughter, Sharman, who was sixteen perhaps at the time. She was debating with herself whether to spend the summer at home doing whatever she wanted to do or going to Florida. She was very interested in animals, and she was going to go down to some place where they work with manatees. Meanwhile, I, the anxious doom-ridden father, dreaded having her take that long drive to Florida by herself and being down there without me to watch over her. I was smart enough not to come out and say that, of course, to her, just smart enough. A few years before I wouldn't have been, I would have said don't do it, but I didn't. But in a hundred ways I indicated indirectly that I didn't want her to go—how much nicer to be at home, the dangers of a long drive for a girl all by herself.

I remember I was sitting in the living room one day when I heard her in the kitchen phoning the manatee people, and I heard her say she'd decided not to come to Florida that summer, that she was going to stay up here and do something else. And then she came back into the living room and plumped herself down on the couch and put her head on my shoulder. In other words, I'd won, but I'd lost. I'd had my will, but I'd kept her from doing something she should have done and could have done and would have enjoyed doing. It was a hollow victory, a sad victory.

So, wars: what does it mean to win, what does it mean to lose? And the wars, of course, against yourself. I certainly am always at war one way or another with myself, and some of them are wars I must fight to try to slay the demons, to kill the dragon, to lay the ghost to rest. But there are other wars you fight with yourself that are really not worth fighting at all. The war to make yourself be more, do more than you have it in you really to do or to be. I think of that wonderful line from one of the poems of my beloved Gerard Manley Hopkins where he says, "My own heart let me more have pity on." My own heart let me more have pity on. That's a lovely phrase. Be merciful to yourself, stop fighting yourself quite so much. Maybe what you are asking of yourself, what you're driving yourself to do or to be, what you put a gun to your own back to make yourself do, is something at this point you needn't have to think about doing. So, think back at the end of the day to the wars you're involved in. How are they going?

And then there's the search for peace. Heaven only knows we're all searching for peace. Peace in terms of the war we fight with ourselves. Peace with the people we love with whom we war. Peace as an alternative to aggressive and defensive actions, snipings, guerrilla warfare. And two things come to my mind: One of them is I have a sister-in-law of whom I've always been very fond, but also she has the capacity for driving me crazy. At her best she is childlike and enchanting, imaginative, fun to be with; at her worst she is childish, egocentric, and difficult— somehow the air bends between her and me. But one day, about two years ago or three, I was sitting beside her at a meal in a restaurant, and I found myself without any premeditation at all telling her about a dream I had about her. "I dreamt about you last night, and the dream was very simple," I said. "I was sitting beside you somewhere, very much like this, and I looked at you in my dream, and I said I love you." And then I said, without premeditation, "And you know that's true." It changed the world. Tears welled up in her eyes. I suppose perhaps they did in mine too, because the truth had been spoken beneath the level of conflict. I did love her, I'd loved her and I was able to tell her that. It not only changed the relationship between her and me, but the waves went out, the ripples went out like when you touch a spider web in any one place the tremor is felt to the furthest reaches of the web, and all sorts of other relationships fell in place. With my brother when we're all together. And she doesn't drive me crazy anymore. When she does the things that used to drive me crazy, I think, well that's just the way she is, and I probably drive her crazy too. Anyway, peace was made between us.

■ ■ ■

And the other thing that I think of when I think of peacemaking is an absolutely devastating scene in Ken Burns's *Civil War* series where you see some shots of the fiftieth anniversary of the Battle of Gettysburg. It was a sort of shaky light and an old grainy film of old men drinking beer and swapping stories and walking over the battlefield fifty years after the terrible battle, and then a voice comes on describing the reenactment of Pickett's Charge. All the old Union veterans, those who were still able to move around, got up on Cemetery Ridge, and all the old Confederate troops who were still able to walk, and the ones that couldn't somebody took them under the arm and helped them, got down on the field they originally marched across. As the description went on, the old Confederates started to march across the field toward the ridge. They gave a couple of rebel yells, and as they did so a moan went up from the old Union troops on the hill, and they rushed down as best they could upon the old Confederate troops, but instead of doing battle they threw their arms around them and hugged them and wept. It was so moving. It took them fifty years to realize that they weren't enemies, but friends. The search for peace; the presence of peace.

And then hunger—the literal hunger of people in the world and our own literal or figurative hunger. What did we hunger for today? Was I fed today? Did I feed anybody today? We all have hidden hungers. We starve without knowing it for each other, I suppose, for silence, for beauty, for holiness, for God. It's the kind of hunger that you don't recognize until it's fed, and then you think, *My golly, I was hungry for that.*

And then homelessness—we're all, by and large, comparatively speaking, rich people and have perhaps more than one home, and yet the question is are we really at home anywhere? Are we really at home in any of our homes? Because it seems to me that to be at home somewhere means to be at peace somewhere, and I have a feeling at some deep level there can really be no real peace for any of us. No real home for any of us until there's some measure of real peace for everybody . . . until everybody has a home. You don't have to be a particularly conscientious or religious person for it to be true of you. I think it's just built into us. We were made by a loving God to love one another, and when we don't, even if we don't think about it and try to look the other way and we see the body in the street in a bag, that other person is part of us. Our peace is threatened by the un-peace of the others. Our homes are not havens when there are so many who have no homes. When we close our eyes to the needs of other people, whether they live on this side of the world or the other side, or under our own roofs, when we close our eyes to their needs, and thus to our own deep needs, we can never really be at home anywhere.

One of Jesus's hard sayings, and one that is rarely mentioned because we're rich relative to many, is: "Woe to you who are rich for you have received your consolation. Woe to you that are full now, for you shall hunger. Woe to you that laugh now, for you shall mourn and weep" (Luke 6:24–26) and woe to us indeed, not only if we forget the poor, but if we forget our own poverty, our own hungers, our own hopelessness and so on.

So it's a way of praying; at least it is a way that's worked sometimes for me to think back over the day for the news of it. What went on, what did God say that day? And then listen to the answer.

And, of course, one of the things we must listen for is joy. It's hard to talk about joy for the almost superstitious reason that you might take the bloom off it, you'll quit, you'll threaten it, you fear it will come to an end when the demons come and gobble it up. But almost in spite of ourselves we get glimpses of joy, and maybe glimpses is all we can ever have of joy. There's a wonderful phrase of Tolkien's in an essay he wrote on fairy tales where he speaks of "Joy beyond the walls of the world, poignant as grief," which you glimpse in fairy tales during what he calls the "sudden joyous 'turn'"—where the frog turns out to be a prince, where the straw is spun into the gold, or the funny little man turns out to be the king, or whatever it is. The sudden glimpse of a joy beyond the walls of the world. We do get glimpses of it, I think, if we have our eyes opened for that possibility, like when I suddenly realized that I was at the manger, or being at SeaWorld where I saw the peaceable kingdom and Eden and tears filled my eyes and also the eyes of my wife and daughter. These glimpses we have of joy—that's part of the news of the day and a very easy part to somehow let slip by.

■ ■ ■

There's one thing I wrote in a book called *Whistling in the Dark* about Advent—if I may choose a favorite liturgical season, it would be Advent—and it suggests something about the elusive glimpses we get of joy.

> The house lights go off and the footlights come on. Even the chattiest stop chattering as they wait in darkness for the curtain to rise. In the orchestra pit, the violin bows are poised. The conductor has raised his baton.
>
> In the silence of a midwinter dusk there is far off in the deeps of it somewhere a sound so faint that for all you can tell it may be only the sound of the silence itself. You hold your breath to listen.
>
> You walk up the steps to the front door. The empty windows at either side of it tell you nothing, or almost nothing. For a second you catch a whiff in the air of some fragrance that reminds you of a place you've never been and a time you have no words for. You are aware of the beating of your heart.

The extraordinary thing that is about to happen is matched only by the extraordinary moment just before it happens. Advent is the name of that moment.

The Salvation Army Santa Claus clangs his bell. The sidewalks are so crowded you can hardly move. Exhaust fumes are the chief fragrance in the air, and everybody is as bundled up against any sense of what all the fuss is really about as they are bundled up against the windchill factor.

But if you concentrate just for an instant, far off in the deeps of you somewhere you can feel the beating of your heart. For all its madness and lostness, not to mention your own, you can hear the world itself holding its breath.[3]

That seems to me to have something to do with what I'm talking about. You've got to be very quiet. Something's about to happen, something is stirring, something holy and precious and beyond words is seeking to be born maybe even in us.

People have asked me about the closures I experienced when I was going through therapy with that lady in Florida. I had that dream about my mother where somehow she seemed back in business and I didn't have to worry about her anymore. But I also received some closure with my father by writing out of the past with my left hand as a way of recapturing the past and having this dialogue with my father who'd been dead for whatever it was, fifty years or so. And that dialogue that I had with him has something to do also with this sort of substratum of joy at the heart of things.

With my left hand I drew pictures with a crayon until I got tired of that and then I just thought I'll see how it comes out. And in this awkward, childish scrawl, using a crayon and a piece of white paper, this dialogue came out between me and my father.

CHILD: How are you?

FATHER: I'm fine.

CHILD: Long time no see.

FATHER: It's been a long time.

CHILD: Do you remember the last time we saw each other, Jamie and I, that morning in November?

FATHER: I remember. You were playing a game. Everybody was asleep.

CHILD: Were you very sad? Were you scared, Daddy? Did you know what you were going to do?

FATHER: I had to do it. Things were so bad there wasn't any good way out.

CHILD: Could I have stopped you, Daddy? If I told you I loved you? If I told you how I needed you?

FATHER: No, nobody could. I was lost so badly.

CHILD: Is this really you I'm talking to? I can't see your face. I've forgotten your voice, your smell.

FATHER: I remember you. I was proud of you. I wanted you to like me.

CHILD: I've been so worried. I've been so scared ever since.

FATHER: Don't be. There's nothing to worry about. That's the secret I never knew, but I know it now.

CHILD: What do you know, Daddy, my dearest dad?

FATHER: I know plenty, and it's all good. I will see you again. Be happy for me. It's my birthday present to you, almost my birthday. I loved you boys. I love you still, child. I love you. Good-bye for now. So long. Everything's going to be all right.

Who's to say what I was in touch with? I'm willing to believe, because the world is full of wonders, that maybe it was my father. Maybe it was some voice within myself, but *there's nothing to worry about. There's nothing to worry about. I know plenty and it's all good.* Maybe that's true. Maybe that is true.

The great George MacDonald, the nineteenth-century novelist and fairy tale writer, in a novel called *Thomas Wingfold, Curate*, writes a speech that is said by the Curate himself, Thomas Wingfold, who was looking back on his years as a minister and sort of summing it up. He says,

> Whatever energies I may or may not have, I know one thing for certain, that I could not devote them to anything else I should think entirely worth doing. Indeed nothing else seems interesting enough—nothing to repay the labour, but the telling of my fellow-men about the one man who is the truth, and to know whom is the life. Even if there be no hereafter, I would live my time believing in a grand thing that ought to be true if it is not. No facts can take the place of truths, and if these be not truths, then is the loftiest part of our nature a waste. Let me hold by the better than the actual, and fall into nothingness off the same precipice with Jesus and John and Paul and a thousand more, who were lovely in their lives, and with their death make even the nothingness into which they have passed like the garden of the Lord. I will go further . . . and say, I would rather die for evermore believing as Jesus believed, than live for evermore believing as those that deny him.[4]

I would rather die for evermore believing as Jesus believed, than live for evermore believing as those that deny him.

I told this story to a group of people at a retreat once, and the morning I told my story I felt quite like being alone for a while, not talking at all. So I went back to my room, and I laid down flat on my bed and tried to do the kind of thing that meditation people tell you. I tried to concentrate my breathing to empty my mind. It worked quite well—I was able to turn off the current of my thoughts. Meditation people also suggest that as you're lying down or sitting, you think of a radar scanning your body bit by bit—your forehead, around your eyes, back of your neck, your head, and as it scans you notice what feelings you have and you say to those parts of your body, *Relax, soften, be still, rest, take it easy.* And I did that bit by bit, and instead of thinking of the radar, I thought of Christ being the one to touch my forehead, eyes, cheeks and neck, my shoulders, so much tension in the back, and so on. By the time I finished, I felt wonderfully relaxed and totally let my body go so that I was heavier than I would normally be. And I thought of that phrase "dead weight." I was a dead weight, and yet I was a live weight too, as if all of the life in me had simply let go and I was supported by the mattress.

And then my image was of being held by whatever there is that is holy to hold us. The image comes from that wonderful part of Moses's psalm. He's dying on the side of Mount Nebo, giving Israel his final blessing, and he says,

> There is none like God . . .
> who rides through the heavens to your help,
> and in his majesty through the skies.
> The eternal God is your dwelling place,
> and underneath are the everlasting arms.
>
> DEUTERONOMY 33:26–27 RSV

I was there lying in my bed with my full weight, every muscle relaxed, and it was as if I were held in those everlasting arms.

Joy is knowing that that is true from your stomach. Knowing that even though you see only through a glass darkly, even though lots of things happen—wars and peacemaking, hunger and homelessness—joy is knowing, even for a moment, that underneath everything are the everlasting arms.

NOTES

1. J. D. Salinger, *Franny and Zooey* (New York: Little, Brown, 2014), 168–70.
2. From *Telling Secrets*, pages 100–102.
3. From *Whistling in the Dark*, pages 2–3.
4. George MacDonald, *Thomas Wingfold, Curate*, http://www .online-literature.com/george-macdonald/thomas-wingfold/75/, accessed 2/20/2017.

A Crazy, Holy Grace

The Healing Power of Pain and Memory

Frederick Buechner

When pain is real, why is God silent?

Frederick Buechner has grappled with the nature of pain, grief, and grace ever since his father committed suicide when Buechner was a young boy. In this essential collection of essays, including one never before published, Frederick Buechner finds that the God who might seem so silent is ever near. He writes about what it means to be a steward of our pain and about this grace from God that seems arbitrary and yet draws us to his care. And he tells about the magic of memory and how it can heal old wounds with memories of past goodnesses and graces from God.

Buechner's best writings on pain and loss, covering such topics as the power of secrets, loss of a loved one, letting go, and resurrection from the ruins, reveal that pain and sorrow can be a treasure—an amazing grace.

Buechner says that loss will come to all of us, but he writes that we are not alone. Crazy and unreal as it may sometimes seem, God's holy, healing grace is always present and available if we are still enough to receive it.

Available in stores and online!

ZONDERVAN®
.com